DEDICATION

This book is dedicated to my families. My family in India, my work family at Nuclear AMRC, my *Bake Off* family – cast, crew and bakers – and my families in Sheffield and Rotherham, in particular the staff at my local supermarkets and Rotherham Leisure Centre.

An Hachette UK Company
www.hachette.co.uk

First published in Great Britain in 2022 by
Kyle Books, an imprint of Kyle Cathie Ltd
Carmelite House
50 Victoria Embankment
London EC4Y 0DZ
www.kylebooks.co.uk

ISBN: 9781914239236

Distributed in the US by Hachette Book Group, 1290 Avenue
of the Americas, 4th and 5th Floors, New York, NY 10104

Distributed in Canada by Canadian Manda Group, 664 Annette St., Toronto, Ontario, Canada M6S 2C8

Publishing Director: Judith Hannam
Publisher: Joanna Copestick
Project Editor: Samhita Foria
Design: Evi O Studio | Susan Le & Wilson Leung
Food styling: Lottie Covell
Props styling: Lydia McPherson
Production Manager: Caroline Alberti

A Cataloguing in Publication record for this title
is available from the British Library

Printed and bound in China

10 9 8 7 6 5 4 3 2 1

SHOWSTOPPING CAKES

RAHUL MANDAL

KYLE BOOKS

**PHOTOGRAPHY BY
MAJA SMEND**

Contents

My baking journey

I made my first cake in 2016 and if you had asked me then whether I would ever write my own baking book, I would have laughed. I grew up in India surrounded by lots of good food. My dad still goes to the market every morning for fresh vegetable and fish, which my mum transforms into something delicious. As a child, I thought there was sorcery happening in the kitchen and whenever I got the chance, I used to watch her cook. Baking, though, didn't feature. Like many other middle-class families in India, we didn't have an oven. My experience of cake was limited to the fruitcakes the local grocery store stocked at Christmas. These usually came wrapped in plastic but there were also more expensive ones in tins. These were the ones my family preferred, as we liked to keep the tins to use as storage for little things.

So how did cake become such a feature in my life? In December 2010 I came to the UK to do a PhD at Loughborough University. It was a big change. Growing up I didn't have friends, but I never felt the lack, as I was surrounded by a large, close-knit family. Coming to Loughborough taught me two important life lessons: how to be a grown-up and how to deal with loneliness. The first lesson I learnt quickly. But I didn't deal very well with loneliness. So, I joined the Gardening Society. It was there I discovered that cakes could be made at home. To see people bringing home-baked biscuits to social events was a revelation!

That Christmas I wanted to give my newly made acquaintances in the Gardening Society presents but as an international student on a grant I had little money. Then Nigella Lawson came to my rescue. She didn't literally come to Loughborough to help me, but she did introduce me to the world of mince pies. Now, don't get too excited: I didn't make the pastry, I bought it. The mincemeat, too, but I added some chopped apples and dried cranberries. They were okay actually. I also made stained-glass cookies. The see-through bit of boiled sweet in the middle was too magical for me to resist. I need to thank Lorraine Pascale for these. She describes them as the perfect Christmas present and wraps hers in cellophane bags. To be really honest, though, I couldn't find any cellophane bags, so I used wrapping paper instead. Two mince pies and two stained glass cookies each. Since then, it has become my Christmas tradition. Every year I make mince pies (and these days, even my own pastry) and stained-glass biscuits. They literally mean Christmas to me.

My life in Loughborough was good, but sometimes you need to stir things up to create space for something new! That stir came when I moved to Rotherham, to take up a research job at the Nuclear Advanced Manufacturing Research Centre (AMRC). Starting again from scratch somewhere else is difficult. My work colleagues did much to make me feel comfortable but I was missing some kind of social life. I joined Rotherham Leisure Centre, and also spent time chatting with the staff at my local supermarket. I know it might sound depressing, but everyone in the leisure centre and the supermarket was super nice, caring and friendly, and I can't thank enough to them for giving me companionship. They unknowingly became part of my social circle, long before *Bake Off*.

Why cake is so special

The first time I baked an actual cake was on my birthday. Birthdays in Bengal are celebrated with rice pudding, so when my parents visited me in 2016, that is what my mum made for me. I thought that as I was celebrating in the UK, why don't I bake a cake? The easiest appeared to be Mary Berry's Victoria sandwich – with cream and jam, of course.

I watched that YouTube video of Mary at least ten times before I started baking. You'd think it would have been fine, but it wasn't. I took the cake to work and one of my colleagues very kindly asked me what temperature and setting I'd baked it at. Little did I know that there were two settings on the oven – fan and normal! As instructed, I'd baked it 180°C but on fan and, as a result, the cake was dark outside and a little raw in the middle. I learned two things that day: read the recipe carefully, every word of it; and at work, everyone loves cake.

A couple of weeks later there was a Macmillan Coffee Morning fundraiser at work, which gave me another opportunity to bake a cake. This time the Victoria sponge was lovely and moist, and I decorated it with cream and fresh fruits... and it tasted nice. Life would be so much simpler if only I had stopped there, but having mastered Victoria sandwich, I thought why not learn how to make buttercream icing? A 20cm (8in) sandwich cake needs a maximum 500–600g (1lb 2oz–1lb 5oz) of icing but I made more than double that amount, which meant that the actual cake was all but invisible. I was given a lift to work that day by my colleague Dawn and it was traumatic for both of us. I can't bring myself to describe either the state of my hands holding the plate or the amount of grainy pink buttercream that slid off! I learnt my third and fourth lessons that day: DO NOT pile cakes with an equal weight of buttercream; and to make a good American buttercream you need to whisk the butter for at least 10 minutes before you add the icing sugar.

After that experience I took a break from baking cakes, but when I heard that other colleagues – Iwona, Ula and Julia – were all pregnant at the same time, I couldn't resist the challenge of baking a cake for them. This is why cake is special, whenever you hear a good news, you think to celebrate it with something sweet... with a cake!

Around this time, I also found out about *Bake Off*. I fell in love with the show instantly and watched all the previous series. Nadiya Hussain's win in 2015 remains, for me, one of the most inspiring moments in television history, especially her winning speech. Thinking about it gives me goosebumps. It was her cake in the final showstopper that inspired the one I made for my colleagues. It was a three-tier lemon drizzle cake with lemon curd and white chocolate ganache, decorated with handmade sugar flowers. Everyone at work was just shocked and the three mothers-to-be were delighted. I think that was the moment when my colleague David suggested I apply for *Bake Off*...

The Great British Bake Off

At first, I didn't take him seriously. But he was persistent and kept asking me if I had applied almost every day, so eventually I applied for the 2017 series. I went through the selection stage okay I guess, but I failed miserably in the telephone interview. When the show aired, we were introduced to some of the most talented bakers I have ever known: Sophie Faldo, Steven Carter-Bailey and Liam Charles. And I said to myself, if I am going to apply again, I will do it properly and get myself prepared! So, the extensive baking research started. I learnt about different bakes and studied recipes during the week and at the weekend I did the baking.

It was like a little science experiment going on in my life. I used to bring the results to my colleagues and to the staff at the local supermarket and leisure centre, who gave me company in my early years in Rotherham. That year I went to David's for Christmas and practised six different puddings for the two nights I stayed. And, according to his wife Liz, I glazed their kitchen floor with sugar syrup! I also took three desserts to a gathering at the house of another of my colleagues, Kathryn. That kind of intense baking experience was great practice for the show.

I could write a whole other book about my experience as a novice amateur baker on *Bake Off*, but let's keep it short and sweet – like a cake – for this one. Suffice to say I learnt a lot more both about baking and myself than ever before. The bakers are now a part of my extended family. They were all brilliant bakers and capable of winning that cake stand any day. This applies to every single baker who has ever been part of *Bake Off*. The amazing team at Love Productions –

producers, home economists, food stylists – were hugely supportive and I am in touch with a lot of them and I know they will be absolutely delighted and super proud to know I have finally written a book!

I was a bit intimidated by Paul Hollywood. But he is an amazing baker. Both he and Prue Leith can just look at a bake and tell you what is wrong with it before even trying it. A lot of the filming doesn't make it to the final episode, but they give loads of brilliant baking tips to all of us while judging and I cannot thank them enough for that.

Finally, I can't end my *Bake Off* reminiscences without mentioning Noel Fielding. He always appeared at my station whenever I was at a crucial stage of getting something done, but somehow we ended up having a completely bonkers chat about absolutely everything for hours. He never tried any of the bakes, but he can make you laugh at the most difficult of times.

What makes a cake work?

I worked full time and although I had the week to research my bakes, I only ever had the weekend to perfect things. If they didn't work, I had to wait another week before I could try again. I therefore did a lot of research into what can guarantee success, as well as into the common tricks, tips and troubleshooting techniques that can salvage any bakes that are not going according to the plan.

Below I've listed some of the key ways to ensure every cake works first time. I've also given tips throughout for specific recipes. It may seem like a lot to remember, but the more you bake the more they will become second nature.

✿ **Always follow a recipe** Until you figure out exactly how it works. Don't attempt to give something your own little twist on your own until you've mastered the basics.

✿ **Preheat your oven** (And check whether it is fan or not!). If the oven is too low, the rising, setting and browning stages of baking will overlap, resulting in a more densley textured cake, often with sunken middle.

✿ **Make sure all the ingredients are at a similar temperature** Especially the fats: (butter and eggs). The most common reason for a cake batter curdling is the difference in the temperature of various fats. Making cake batter not only incorporates air into the mix, it also emulsifies the ingredients to a homogenous batter. If the fats are different temperatures, they won't combine and the mixture curdles.

✿ **Line your baking tins properly** Rub the inside with a bit of butter using kitchen towel, then sprinkle with a tablespoon of flour and rotate the tin so all sides are evenly coated. This often is sufficient to ensure smooth sides, but I always line the sides and base of the tin with baking paper too.

✿ **Measure your ingredients correctly** Eyeballing ingredients can often result in a not-so-great bake. If a recipe specifies 1 teaspoon of baking powder (normally 5g/⅛oz), but you just went rogue and spooned in double this amount, the cake will rise too quickly and then sink in the middle. So, please, measure the ingredients correctly.

✿ **Check the baking time** Recipes usually don't give a precise baking time. The reason is that the heat distribution in your oven and the thickness and material of your baking tin all play a role in how long your sponge needs to be baked for. It might all sounds a bit confusing, but fear not, there are some easy ways to know when your cake is ready. First, when the cake is done, it will come away from the sides of the tin and needs to be taken out of the oven. Also, if you gently touch the sponge (please be careful not to burn your finger!) it will spring back. If you are still unsure, take a skewer or cocktail stick and insert it into the middle of the sponge. If the sponge is baked properly the skewer should come out clean.

Baking techniques

It may seem like I am throwing a lot of things at you without explaining why we need to be mindful about them. To understand that you need to know how cake batter is prepared and baked. The aim of preparing any cake batter is to incorporate air in the batter, which will expand during baking to provide its light and spongy texture. A pound cake or sandwich cake usually has equal amounts of four key ingredients – butter, sugar, eggs and flour – plus optional flavouring. So the achieve the perfect batter you first weigh the eggs (including the shell) and then measure the same weight of butter, sugar and flour. The main job of butter is to provide richness, and sugar, the sweetness. The eggs and flour contribute to the overall structure of the cake. Below are the main methods of preparing cake batter:

CREAMING METHOD

In this method, the butter and sugar are creamed (by which I mean beaten) together for 5–7 minutes using an electric whisk until really pale and fluffy. This is the principal/most important stage when making a cake using this method. The action of beating the butter and sugar together incorporates air, which makes the batter lighter in colour and fluffier in texture. (If you want to prove this, drop a bit of batter after creaming it for 7 minutes into a bowl of cold water and it will float.) Then scrape down the sides of the bowl and whisk for a further couple of minutes to ensure that every bit of butter and sugar is incorporated. After that, add one egg at a time and whisk until the egg is emulsified properly with the batter.

The temperature of the eggs and butter is crucial at this stage. Ideally, they should be the same. Easiest is to take the butter out of the fridge the night before you want to make the sponges. If the temperature of the butter is different from that of the eggs, it causes curdling during emulsification. It is best to avoid this situation if possible. However, if it does happen, add a tablespoon of flour and whisk in after the addition of each egg. The batter will become smoother in no time.

This brings us to the next ingredient: flour. Often recipes specify self-raising flour, which is plain flour premixed with baking powder. Baking powder is a combination of sodium bicarbonate and a dried acid, such as cream of tartar (potassium bitartrate). In its dry condition, it is inert, meaning it doesn't react. But when added to the batter, the liquid from the batter makes it active, creating lots of tiny carbon dioxide bubbles which fill the cake batter. To give maximum flexibility, commercial baking powders often have a two-stage rise – once during mixing, and again during oven baking. Ingredients lists for all-in-one methods will include baking powder. If you opt to use the creaming method and the recipe specifies the all-in-one method, you do not need to add any baking powder.

Flour contains protein and carbohydrate in the form of gluten and starch respectively. The protein gives structure to a cake. During baking, the carbohydrate molecules swell as they absorb the liquid in the batter and form a gel that supports the protein strands and stabilises the cake. For bread you need a flour with a high gluten content because the dough needs to be elastic. When you knead dough you work on the gluten, which forms the distinctive bread structure. For cake, however, you want the exact opposite, so it is better to handle the batter as little as possible, which is why recipes tell you to 'fold in' the flour. (I often sieve it on top of the creamed butter-sugar-egg mix and fold it in with a quick but gentle motion.)

The batter is now ready to be baked. If you are making this cake with 3–4 medium free-range eggs, choose two 20cm (8in) baking tins. This allows enough time for the cakes to rise and the structures to stablise without over-browning the top. You can of course scrape the batter into a single deep 20cm (8in) tin but if you do so you need to reduce the temperature by 10°C (18°F) and bake it for longer. It will all make sense if I explain what happens during the actual baking.

A lot of reactions happen in the oven, all of them induced by heat. We can break these down into three generalised stages: expansion or rising; setting the structure; and colouring.

Expansion is the stage when the batter reaches its full volume. The heat from the oven makes the trapped gases – air or carbon dioxide – expand in volume. Volume increases in direct proportion to absolute temperature (assuming constant pressure), just as with every other gas. This is what gives us the familiar aerated texture. Alongside this expansion, the water molecules start to evaporate and create steam, which also expands and increases the total volume of the bake.

During the setting stage, the structural elements of egg and flour start to form the structure of the bake. The coiled protein molecules (gluten) start to denature or unwind, and coagulate or firm up. The starch molecules absorb water and swell until they disrupt and gelate. Along with the coagulated protein, this is what gives the cake its final spongy structure.

In the final colouring stage, the batter shape becomes stable. The proteins and sugars react to the direct heat on the surface of the bake to create a golden crust. This is known as the Maillard reaction, which, at higher temperatures, results in caramelisation. The Maillard reaction can create hundreds of different flavour compounds depending on the conditions and ingredients – the same basic reaction also gives roasted coffee and seared meat their distinctive flavours.

All of these heat-induced reactions mean that when you are baking a lot of batter in one cake tin, the colouring stage happens before, not after, the setting stage. As a result, the cake will get a darker crust.

ALL-IN-ONE METHOD

In the all-in-one method, the air is incorporated by the action of baking powder, so the ingredients lists for cakes made using this method will always include baking powder. The texture achieved by this method will be similar but creaming introduces a lot more air into the batter, and the the overall height of the all-in-one cake will be a bit less in comparison. I often sacrifice both texture and height for ease and flexibility.

WHISKED SPONGES

The whisking method creates light-as-a-feather sponges. There are two main types: fatless sponges and those that include fat. The main ingredients for whisked sponges are eggs, sugar and flour – usually 25–30g (1oz) sugar, plus the same quatity of flour per egg (depending on the size of the eggs). For fatless sponges, you whisk the eggs and sugar at very high speed for 7–10 minutes, which results in a tripling of the volume of the batter. The point when this is achieved is called the ribbon stage: as you lift up the whisk the batter drops from it like a ribbon and sits on the top of the batter in the bowl for at least 10 seconds before disappearing. You definitely need an electric whisk or a stand mixer for this method. During the whisking, the protein molecules, which are usually strangled with each other in eggs, get separated and denatured. When they are combined with sugar molecules they create a foam, trapping lots of air inside. Whisking while the bowl is set on top of a pan of simmering water (bain-marie) speeds up the process, as the heat helps the protein molecules in eggs get denatured faster.

As there is no added leavening agent, it is important to keep as much air possible in the batter, so when you fold in the sifted flour, try to do so really gently. To add richness and flavour you can fold melted butter into the batter, in which case is it called a Genoise sponge.

MERINGUE-BASED SPONGES

Another way to introduce air into cake batter is to fold meringue into a batter or to fold nut flour into a meringue.

Meringues are a mixture of egg whites and sugar. When you whisk egg whites, they become foamy as the coiled protein molecules untangle, but the foam will collapse after a while. The addition of sugar transforms the fragile foam into stable, glossy meringue. The more sugar you add, the more stable the meringue becomes, though you shouldn't add more than 50–55g (1¾–2oz) per egg white. After the meringue cloud has formed, it can either be folded into a mixture of egg yolk, flour and butter, as in joconde and chiffon cakes, or ground nuts can be folded into the meringue, in which case it becomes a dacquoise. Depending on the baking time, meringue can have a wide variety of textures.

As most of the structure, as well as the air, is provided from the meringue, these types of sponges can easily be made gluten free.

COOLING SPONGES

Once baked, sponges should be left to cool in the tin on a wire rack for at least 5–10 minutes. This is because when first out of the oven, sponges are still quite delicate. If you try to take them out of the tin straightaway you can easily break them. After 10 minutes, remove them carefully and place on the wire rack to cool completely.

Often, people place a sponge in the fridge to cool it quickly. Please try to avoid this as it makes the sponge drier as it cools. If you really do need to cool it quickly, first wrap it in clingfilm before putting in the fridge or preferably the freezer.

STORING SPONGES

Once cooled, wrap the sponges in clingfilm and store in the fridge for few days or in the freezer for up to a week. For the sponges stored in the freezer let them defrost in the fridge overnight before using as normal.

ASSEMBLING A CAKE

There are three main types of cake assembly:

✿ Naked and semi-naked cakes
✿ Fully frosted cakes
✿ Tiered cakes

Whichever you're doing, make sure you have your fillings and frosting ready before you start.

NAKED AND SEMI-NAKED CAKES

Naked cake assembly requires the least effort and is great for beginners. It involves the layering of sponges with fillings of your choice and that's it. Ideally, of course, your sponges have smooth sides. This is easy enough to achieve if you line the bottom and sides of the cake tin with baking paper. You can add a bit of glamour by piping the filling between layers instead of spreading it. Place the first layer on a cake board or turntable. Spoon the filling into a piping bag, then slowly rotate the board/table as you pipe the filling. Repeat this process until all the layers are stacked.

Semi-naked cakes are a little more challenging. They are assembled in a similar way to a naked cake, but then at the end coated with a single layer of buttercream. This first layer of buttercream coating is called the crumb coat, as you do this to adhere any loose crumbs to the surface of the cake and make it look nice and smooth.

FULLY FROSTED CAKES

These are a level higher than the semi-naked cakes and a turntable and a cake scraper are extremely useful. After crumb coating a cake, you place it in the fridge for 30–45 minutes or in the freezer for 15–20 minutes for the buttercream to set. Then you take the cake out of the fridge/freezer and coat with a generous portion of buttercream using a palette knife. Once coated with the second layer of buttercream, rotate the turntable in a steady motion while touching the cake scraper at a right angle to the surface of the cake. The cake scraper will scrape the excess buttercream from the sides of the cake leaving a smooth straight surface.

However, you don't have to always go for the smooth sharp buttercream finish if you don't wish to. It is easy to decorate the sides of the cakes with fruits, berries, nuts, meringues or even with some casual strokes of a spoon.

TIERED CAKES

These are definitely the most challenging, but also the most rewarding too. I am often asked: how do you know when you are ready to make a tier cake?

My answer is: you're always ready! If you can bake a sponge, you can make a tier cake very easily. You can even tier up two naked or semi-naked cakes and I guarantee they will look fantastic.

The most important consideration is the stability of the structure. For dense cakes, like fruitcake, you might not need internal dowel support, but for lighter sponge cakes dowel supports are essential. The steps below will help you:

✿ Always ensure all the tiers are on individual cake boards that match the size of the sponges.

✿ Make sure you have all the cakes ready and frosted (unless you want them naked) and prepare some extra frosting to cover the joins either by piping or arranging decorations across the join of the two cakes.

✿ Use a minimum of four dowels. These can be either wooden or plastic according to preference, but remember it helps if the dowel is reasonably thick.

✿ Imagine a square slightly smaller than the top tier. (For a 15cm/6in top tier, you need to imagine a 10cm/4in square.) Insert the first dowel in one of the corners of the imaginary square in the base tier. Measure with an edible marker and cut the excess dowel with sharp scissors.

✿ Use this excess part of the dowel as a guide to cut lengths from the remaining three dowels. Insert them at the remaining corners of the imaginary square.

✿ Spread a thin layer of frosting to cover the top of the dowels and place in the fridge to set.

✿ Once set, take the base tier out of the fridge and place on the final cake stand. Carefully lift and place the top tier on the base tier making sure the base of the top tier is centred on the dowels, which will ensure that the weight of the tier above is not on the base tier sponges, but on the dowel supports.

✿ Pipe the frosting across the joint or junction of the cake. This step is optional, but this little effort will make your cake look a lot neater and prettier.

✿ Repeat as necessary for any further tiers.

Ingredients

❀ **Eggs** Not just used whole for sponges, egg whites are also used for meringues, royal icing and buttercreams, and egg yolks for pastry crème. It is always worth using good quality eggs – I prefer to use free-range. The yolks are so much more yellow, which gives the crumb a beautiful golden hue.

❀ **Butter** I prefer to use unsalted butter in cakes. For buttercreams, though, you can use a combination of salted and unsalted butter if you don't have enough unsalted butter in stock. Pretty much all cakes and buttercream require soft-to-touch, room temperature butter. If you forget to take it out of the fridge in time to achieve this, place the butter on a microwave-safe plate and microwave on a medium setting for no more than 10 seconds.

❀ **Oil** I use butter for most cakes but some are easier to make with oil. Unless I am making a cake that requires a flavoured oil, I use sunflower oil.

❀ **Baking spread.** If you want, you can replace butter with a baking spread, but remember that baking spreads have a higher percentage of water than butter, so you may not need to use the additional milk to loosen the cake. Also please NEVER use baking spread for buttercreams.

❀ **Flour** There are two types used in cake making:

> **Plain** (*all-purpose*) flour contains 8–11% gluten and is perfect for making cakes. Flours that contain more gluten will make a sponge that is a bit tight and chewy.

> **Self raising** (*self-rising*) flour is plain flour with added baking powder and is what I use in all my recipes. If it is unavailable, you can make your own by adding 5g (⅛oz) of baking powder to every 100g (3½oz) of plain flour being used.

❀ **Baking powder.** When added to a batter, baking powder activates in the liquid, creating lots of tiny carbon dioxide bubbles which fill the cake batter, allowing it to rise.

❀ **Sugar** Sugar adds all-important sweetness to cakes, jams, crèmes etc, and comes in various forms:

> **Caster** (*superfine*) sugar has tiny granules which means it gets mixed with butter faster and traps a lot of air during creaming.

> **Brown** sugar comes in light and dark varieties and has a slight caramel flavour.

> **Icing** (*confectioner's*) sugar is finely ground sugar with a little cornstarch added and is perfect for icing thanks to its light and fluffy texture.

> **Jam** sugar is caster sugar with added pectin. As the name suggests it is perfect for making jams and preserves. The pectin helps the jam to set quicker.

❀ **Milk** I strongly recommend using full fat (*whole*) milk, particularly when making pastry crème. If it's only being used to loosen the cake batter, semi-skimmed can be used.

❀ **Cream** I mostly prefer to use double (*heavy*) cream as its fat content of 33% gives it enough body to whisk and use as a filling for cakes, ganache, making mousses etc. However, if you prefer you can use whipping cream or a 50:50 mix of double and whipping cream.

❀ **Spices** (roasted, crushed, ground). I use a lot of spices in my baking and would always recommend first roasting them to release the oil and then crushing or grinding them to gain the maximum flavour. However, for ease, shop-bought ground spices are okay.

❀ **Chocolate** I mostly use dark and white chocolate. For dark chocolate anything between 50 and 75% cocoa solids is good. In cakes or buttercream, supermarket own-brand chocolate is fine but for tempering (page 75) and making chocolate decorations having tempered chocolate pellets does help.

❀ **Food colouring** I prefer to use gels as they are more concentrated than other varieties so you only need to use a little amount. To get a uniform distribution in cake batter, mix the gel with a couple of tablespoons of milk, then pour into the batter and whisk. To avoid the colour speckling in buttercream, either mix the gel with a bit of vanilla extract or with a tablespoon of milk and whisk in. Otherwise, you can use oil-based food colouring. For colouring white chocolate, always use oil-based food colouring.

✿ **Citrus fruits** I am huge fan of citrus. Lemon, oranges, limes, grapefruit, yuzu... I use everything. The flavour of citrus comes from its juice and also from the zest. Personally, I prefer to add flavour to bakes using zested citrus rather than lemon or orange extract.

✿ **Fruits and berries** Fruits are nature's gift that should be incorporated into bakes more. I use them generously. One tip I got from Paul Hollywood is to use frozen berries rather than fresh within batters as they retain the right texture as you bake and don't turn to mush when cooked.

Equipment

- **Electric hand whisk** Along with digital scales, this is the most important piece of baking equipment and can be used to make pretty much every single cake batter, meringue and buttercream in this book. When making bigger batches of cake and buttercream, you will need to do things in batches.

- **Stand mixer** This is the absolute dream for any home baker, but can be expensive. If you bake regularly, maybe this can be your Christmas present to yourself!

- **Digital weighing scales** An absolute necessity for any baker. Usually a set will last for ages, though from time to time you will need to change the batteries.

- **Digital thermometer** I first bought mine for tempering chocolate, but now use it for making jams, as well as Swiss and Italian meringues.

- **Stainless-steel saucepans** You might find me old school, but stainless-steel saucepans are perfect for baking related activities. As an example, when making caramel, we often judge the richness by observing the deep amber colour, which cannot be seen properly if using a non-stick saucepan.

- **Heatproof and microwave-safe bowls** You need a couple of such bowls to do everything from melting chocolate in a bain-marie to warming cream in microwave.

- **Silicone spatulas** These are essential for scraping the last bit of cake batter out of the bowl.

- **Good-sized mixing bowl**

- **Turntable** This is used for icing and decorating the cakes.

- **A measuring spoon set**

- **Measuring jug**

- **Baking sheets and baking trays**

- **Cake tins** *(pans).* Loose-bottom cake tins are my preference. I have a good selection of 20cm (8in), 15cm (6in) and 10cm (4in) circular and square cake tins. These are the main sizes I use throughout the book.

- **Piping bags, piping nozzle coupler and piping nozzles** These are must-have if you like cake decorating.

- **Fridge/freezer space** Many of these cakes need to be set in the frigde or freezer.

- **Palette knife** One of these broad, flexible blades is extremely useful for coating and spreading buttercream on cakes.

- **Offset palette knife (big and small)** Very useful for spreading cake batter, buttercream, ganache, etc onto cake or on baking paper.

- **Cake scraper** This is essential if you want to have smooth-sided cakes.

- **Baking paper** For lining cake tins/ baking sheets.

- **Skewers.** To check if the cakes are done.

- **Acetate sheet and acetate roll** These are not absolutely necessary but they are very useful while doing tempered chocolate/candy melt decorations. They result in a very smooth surface for chocolate.

- **Dowels** For making tiered cakes.

- **Balloon whisks** These are extremely handy for whisking ganache, cream or pastry crème.

- **Plunger cutters** For making marzipan flowers and decorations.

Tips and solutions to common problems

✿ **The cake has sunk in the middle** Probably the most common problem encountered. If you have followed a recipe correctly, it shouldn't happen, but if it does check the temperature of your oven. If it is too high when the cakes are put in, air and gases trapped in the cake will expand faster and escape before the protein and starch have had time to coagulate and form a gel.
As a result, the cake will sink in the middle.

   The other reason could be the use of an extra leavening agent like baking powder, which will cause the cake to sink for the same reason, as the gases will be produced and expanded before the cake structure sets.

   Also, please don't open the door of the oven while the cake is baking, as it will make the pressure and temperature in the oven drop and thus interrupt the rising process.

✿ **Cake mixture curdling** If the fats being used (butter, oil, eggs, etc) are not all the same temperature, they will not emulsify to a homogenous batter. If your batter has curdled, fold in a tablespoon of sifted flour. If your batter has curdled while using the creaming method, fold in a tablespoon of sifted flour after the addition of each egg. For the all-in-one method, you can't do much about it. Bake it as usual, the resulting cake might have a lower height.

✿ **Colouring sponges** These are often a delight to make, especially for kids. Always use concentrated gel food colouring, mix with 1–1½ tablespoons of milk and then whisk into the batter. Coloured sponges can have a tendency to be slightly dry, which can be avoided byadding a couple of tablespoons of room-temperature yogurt into the batter and whisking it through.

✿ **Fruits sinking to the bottom** The best way to avoid this, is to toss the fruits in a couple of tablespoons of flour before incorporating them into the batter. This applies to dried, fresh and frozen fruits.

✿ **Grainy American buttercream** The main cause of American buttercream being grainy is not whisking the butter for long enough and not sifting the icing sugar. First you need to start with soft (but not oily) room-temperature butter. Whisk it for at least 7–8 minutes, scraping the sides from time to time. Make sure the colour of the whisked butter has changed to almost cream. Then sift in half the icing sugar and beat well for another 4–5 minutes. Finally add the rest of the icing sugar along with any flavouring and whisk for a further 5–7 minutes. Remember to scrape down the sides of the bowl to incorporate all the butter and sugar.

✿ **Italian and Swiss meringue buttercream** The main issue with making these buttercreams is that they tend to reach a 'soupy' stage before becoming spreadable. I am afraid the only solution is to be patient and keep the mixer or whisk going while adding butter. It will come together at the end. But always remember to start adding butter when the meringue is at room temperature. If it is a hot day, it can remain soupy for longer, so you can quickly pop the mixing bowl in the fridge for 10-15 minutes to cool it and then start whisking again. It should get to the spreadable consistency faster.

✿ **Storage of excess buttercream** I would say buttercream can be stored in a plastic container on the kitchen worktop overnight, in the fridge for a couple of days or in the freezer for a few months. Always defrost before use. After defrosting, or if taken

Introduction

straight from the fridge, melt a couple of tablespoons of your buttercream in a microwave and add it to the rest in a bowl. Then whisk for 4–5 minutes to achieve a soft and spreadable texture.

✿ **Ganache that is too hard** If you chill the ganache in the fridge for too long it will set hard in the bowl. Please do not try to reheat it, either in a microwave or on the hob, as it is extremely easy to split it while doing so. Take it out of the fridge and chop it up. Then heat it in a heatproof bowl over a pan of simmering water until it softens. If it is still too hard after whisking, add a couple of tablespoons of warm water or cream and whisk again to get a spreadable consistency.

✿ **Ganache splitting** To make chocolate ganache, you warm the cream until it is just about to boil, take it off the heat and add chopped chocolate or pour over chopped chocolate, then let it sit for about 5 minutes, before whisking. If the cream is too hot, then the ganache tends to split. If it does, whisk in a couple of tablespoons of cold cream. It will slowly come back to smoothness.

✿ **If you have time always drizzle your cake with a bit of syrup** Drizzling with syrup improves even moist cakes and can transform those that are dry. Use equal amounts of sugar and water to make your syrup and add flavourings such as vanilla, citrus juice and zest and spices.

Flavour pairing

Making a good sponge and layering with frosting and filling is only one part of making a cake. At the end of the day, you want it to taste good, and that's where flavour pairing comes into action. Every element of a cake – sponges, drizzles, fillings and frostings – gives you the opportunity to introduce flavour.

The most-used flavour in any cake is probably vanilla, which comes in the form of pods, pastes and cheaper extracts. Once I had tried seeds scraped from a real vanilla pod, it was hard to go back to using extract but pods are very expensive. So these days I often go for the middle ground and use vanilla bean paste.

Another flavour that frequently appears in my recipes is citrus. With citrus I think there is only one way to go – use the zest whenever possible. As an example, if you are making a lemon cake, I would suggest using lemon zest in the sponge, syrup made with lemon juice in the drizzle, lemon curd as a filling and lemon buttercream as a frosting. It will be a true lemon delight.

The flavour of fruit and berries can also be introduced directly in the sponges. If you are baking sponges with berries, frozen is better than fresh, otherwise you can use freeze-dried berries in the sponge, as well as in buttercream to enhance the flavours of the fresh berries.

As I grew up in India, it's no surprise that I like to use spices. Cinnamon is probably the most common spice in baking and can be combined with apples and pears as well as citrus like orange to enhance the flavours of the fruit like a warm hug on a chill autumn evening. I also love cardamom. It has an earthy vanilla-like note with a hint of citrus, which makes it ideal in sponges, fillings and buttercreams. Cardamom can also be paired with flavours such as citrus, berries and chocolate to enrich the flavour profile and give your cake a more complex multi-layered eating experience.

There is no right or wrong way of developing and understanding flavours and flavour combinations. It's key not to be scared of experimenting. Some pairings will work and others will be less popular, but this is the best way to learn! The chart opposite lists the flavour pairings that I like and should be used as a starting point for you to experiment.

Things to pair with	Fruit and berries	Spices and herbs	Nuts	Chocolate and caramel
Lemon	Raspberry, blueberry, blackcurrant, blackberry, redcurrant, strawberry, orange, passion fruit, plum, cherry, apple, rhubarb	Vanilla, cardamom, ginger, mint, poppy seed, thyme, rosemary, basil, aniseed, fennel seed	Almond, pistachio	White chocolate, caramel
Orange	Apple, blackberry, lemon, grapefruit, pear, apricot	Cardamom, vanilla, cinnamon, nutmeg, ginger, star anise, basil, mint	Hazelnut, almond, pecan, pistachio, peanut, coconut	Dark chocolate, milk chocolate, White chocolate, caramel
Lime	Strawberry, pineapple, apple, kiwi, mango, orange, grapefruit	Cardamom, vanilla, star anise, ginger, thyme, basil, mint, chilli	Hazelnut, pecan, coconut	Dark chocolate, white chocolate, Caramel
Apple	Blackberry, blackcurrant, plum, citrus, cranberry, apricot	Cinnamon, cardamom, ginger, vanilla, clove, anise, tarragon	Almond, hazelnut, walnut	Caramel, milk chocolate
Pear	Citrus, plum, blackberry, raspberry	Vanilla, ginger, cardamom, nutmeg	Almond, hazelnut, pecan, peanut	Dark chocolate, caramel
Passion fruit	Kiwi, mango, orange, pineapple, strawberry, lemon, lime	Vanilla, ginger, cardamom, chilli	Almond, hazelnut, pistachio, coconut, peanut	Dark chocolate, milk chocolate, white chocolate, caramel
Cherry	Lemon, orange, plum	Vanilla, cardamom, ginger, fennel	Almond, hazelnut, coconut	Dark chocolate, milk chocolate
Mango	Lemon, orange, lime, kiwi, raspberry, strawberry, pineapple, pomegranate	Vanilla, cardamom, chilli, ginger, nutmeg, mint, basil	Almond, cashew, pistachio, coconut, hazelnut	Dark chocolate, caramel, white chocolate
Raspberry	Lemon, lime, mango, orange, pear, rhubarb	Vanilla, cinnamon, fennel, star anise, tarragon, thyme, mint	Almond, pistachio, pecan, peanut, coconut	Dark chocolate, white chocolate

1

FILLINGS AND FROSTINGS

Buttercream

AMERICAN BUTTERCREAM

Ingredients

200g (7oz) salted butter,
  at room temperature
400g (14oz) icing (confectioner's)
  sugar, sifted
2 teaspoons vanilla bean paste
1–2 tablespoons double (heavy)
  cream
  (you can add extra if the
  buttercream is too stiff)

Variations

You can easily flavour this buttercream
with different extracts and ground spices.

✿ Lemon buttercream: add 1½ teaspoons
lemon extract

✿ Orange buttercream: add
1½-2 teaspoons orange extract

✿ Coconut and cardamom buttercream:
add 1 teaspoon coconut extract and
1½ teaspoons ground cardamom

✿ Raspberry/strawberry buttercream:
add 3–5 tablespoons raspberry/strawberry
jam and whisk thoroughly

✿ Dark/white chocolate buttercream:
replace half the icing sugar with the
equivalent weight of dark/white chocolate
(melted and cooled to room temperature)
and add in step 3

Along with flavourings, it is easy to colour
buttercream with liquid gel food colouring.
Add few drops of food colouring and whisk
to get the desired colour.

Makes enough to coat and fill a two-tier, 20cm (8in) cake

This is the most commonly used type of buttercream and
also the easiest to make. It's great for filling and coating
cakes; it might be overly sweet, but paired with the right
cake and a sharp filling, such as lemon curd, it can be
absolutely delicious. The key part in the buttercream is,
of course, the butter. Make sure it is at room temperature
before you begin: you want it to be soft, but not oily.
If you have a cold block of butter and no time to let it
soften naturally, the easiest thing to do is to microwave
it on a medium setting for no more than 10 seconds.

Method

1   Place the butter in a mixing bowl and whisk for 5–7 minutes
    using an electric whisk, pausing occasionally to scrape down
    the sides of the bowl. T he colour of the butter will change from
    light yellow to cream as you are whisking.

2   Once the butter is well whisked, add half the sifted icing sugar.
    Whisk at a low speed to avoid a cloud of sugar filling your
    kitchen. Once the sugar and butter begin to combine,
    you can whisk at full power for a couple of minutes.

3   Scrape down the sides of the bowl, then add the rest
    of the icing sugar and whisk for another 2 minutes.

4   Finally, add the vanilla and 1 tablespoon of the cream. Whisk
    again until well combined. If you feel that your buttercream
    is too stiff to be spreadable, add another tablespoon of cream
    and whisk to loosen.

FRENCH BUTTERCREAM

Ingredients

190g (6¾oz) caster (super fine) sugar
60ml (4 tablespoons) water
6 large free-range egg yolks
100g (3½oz) salted butter
  (room temperature, cubed)
200g (7oz) unsalted butter
  (room temperature, cubed)
2 teaspoons vanilla bean paste

Makes enough to coat and fill a two-tier, 20cm (8in) cake

This is the most decadent of all buttercreams: rich, velvety
and smooth. The egg yolks add to the creaminess.

Method

1   Place the sugar and water in a small saucepan over a medium
    heat and bring to the boil. Use a thermometer to check
    the temperature. You need to bring the temperature
    to 116°C (240°F).

2   As the temperature of the sugar approaches 110°C (230°F),
    start whisking the egg yolks using an electric whisk.

Fillings and frostings

Again, you can flavour this buttercream, using any extracts or ground spices. It is often used to layer classic chocolate and coffee opera cake.

✿ Coffee French buttercream: mix 3 tablespoons instant coffee powder with 1 tablespoon water to make a paste. Whisk it in with the buttercream

✿ Raspberry/strawberry French buttercream: add 3-4 tablespoons ground freeze-dried raspberries or strawberries and whisk thoroughly

✿ Dark/white chocolate French buttercream: add 200g (7oz) dark/white chocolate (melted and cooled to room temperature) and whisk for 2 minutes

3 When the sugar is at 116°C, add the sugar syrup in a steady stream to the whisked egg yolks, while whisking continuously.

4 Keep whisking until the bowl is cool to the touch.

5 Once the bowl/egg yolk sugar mix is cool to touch, start adding the butter, one cube at a time. Keep it whisking in the medium speed.

6 Once all the butter is added, whisk in the high speed for about 5 minutes, until the buttercream gets a spreadable consistency.

7 Scrape down the sides of the bowl and add the vanilla. Whisk for a further minute to combine.

ITALIAN MERINGUE BUTTERCREAM

Ingredients

150g (5½oz) caster (superfine) sugar
60ml (4 tablespoons) water
3 large free-range egg whites
125g (4½oz) salted butter
   (room temperature, cubed)
250g (9oz) unsalted butter
   (room temperature, cubed)
2 teaspoons vanilla bean paste

Makes enough to coat and fill a two-tier, 20cm (8in) cake

This is a very luxurious buttercream. It is not overly sweet and has a beautiful mouthfeel. On a hot summer's day when all the other types of buttercreams will start to melt, this will stay up! That is why I used this buttercream for most of my cakes in the big white tent.

Method

1 Place the sugar and water in a small saucepan over a medium heat and bring to the boil.

2 Use a thermometer to check the temperature of the syrup. As the temperature of the sugar mixture approaches 110°C (230°F), start whisking the egg whites at high speed in a large bowl using an electric whisk until they form soft peaks.

3 When the sugar syrup reaches 120°C (248°F), take it off the heat and pour it into the whisked egg whites in a steady stream, whisking continuously in high speed. Keep whisking until the bowl is cool to the touch. You will end up with a stiff and shiny Italian meringue.

4 Scrape down the sides of the bowl and start adding the butter, a cube at a time, whisking continuously at medium speed. Once all the butter is incorporated, add the vanilla and scrape down the sides of the bowl once more. Whisk at the highest speed for a couple of minutes until you have a smooth and spreadable buttercream.

Tips

Like American or French buttercream, you can easily flavour this with different extracts, such as lemon, orange, almond, peppermint or rose. You can also add ground spices, such as cinnamon, cardamom, fennel, or star anise.

While colouring the buttercream, try to use oil-based food colouring, it blends with buttercream a lot more homogenously than the normal water-soluble food colouring. But if using the normal water-soluble gel food colouring, mix it with a tablespoon of milk and then whisk into the buttercream for a uniform blend.

SWISS MERINGUE BUTTERCREAM

Ingredients

3 large free-range egg whites

225g (8oz) caster (confectioner's)
  sugar

60ml (4 tablespoons) water

150g (5½oz) salted butter
  (room temperature, cubed)

200g (7oz) unsalted butter
  (room temperature, cubed)

2 teaspoons vanilla bean paste

Tips

Colour and flavour this buttercream exactly
in the same way how you treat French
or Italian meringue buttercream.

When using a stand mixer, remember to
switch to a paddle attachment before you
start to add the butter. If you use the whisk
attachment as the butter goes in, it will end
up giving you a very foamy mouthfeel.

If you see the mixture turning soupy,
be patient and keep whisking. It should
come to a spreadable consistency. There
are few things you can do to prevent
or troubleshoot this situation:

✿ Make sure the bowl is cool to the touch
before you start adding butter.

✿ If the buttercream still remains soupy
after whisking for 10-15 minutes, chill
the buttercream with the bowl in the
fridge for 20-30 minutes. It will bring the
temperature down and when you whisk
after that, it should start to come together.

Makes enough to coat and fill a two-tier, 20cm (8in) cake

This is an easier version of meringue-based buttercream.
However, it tastes equally delicious. Again, it is not
overly sweet, and an excellent option for coating and
filling any cakes. On a day-to-day basis I mostly use
this buttercream. It is easy to pipe decoratively.

Method

1   Add the egg whites and caster sugar to a heatproof bowl set
    over a pan of simmering water. Whisk using a balloon whisk
    until the sugar has melted and is incorporated into the egg
    whites (this should happen at about 65°C/149°F). To check, just
    take a bit of the mix and rub it between your fingers; it should
    not feel gritty at all.

2   Take the bowl off the heat and start whisking using an electric
    whisk. Alternatively, if you have a stand mixer, transfer the
    mixture to your stand mixer and whisk using the whisk
    attachment. Continue to whisk for 7–10 minutes, or until
    you have a shiny, glossy meringue. To check, lift the whisk
    out of the mixture: it should leave a stiff speak.

3   Scrape down the sides of the bowl using a spatula and whisk
    for another few minutes until the bowl is cool to the touch.
    If using a stand mixer, change the whisk attachment to the paddle
    attachment and start mixing again at a medium speed. If using
    an electric whisk, there is no need to change the attachment.

4   With the mixer still running, start adding the butter, a few cubes
    at a time. It may look as if it is turning soupy, but keep going.

5   Once all the butter is incorporated, increase the speed to the
    highest setting and whisk for few minutes more. You should
    end up with a nice, spreadable consistency. Scrape down the
    sides of the bowl and add the vanilla, then mix again at high
    speed to combine.

Cheese-based frosting

MASCARPONE FROSTING

Ingredients

250g (9oz) mascarpone
50g (1¾oz) icing (confectioner's)
  sugar, sifted
300ml (10½fl oz) double (heavy)
  cream
2 teaspoons vanilla extract

Variations

This is easy to flavour with any flavourings like lemon, orange, vanilla, or ground spices like cardamom, cinnamon, or nutmeg.

You can colour it with normal gel food colouring if you wish.

Transform this frosting to a fruit-flavoured mascarpone filling by whisking in 3–4 tablespoons jam or curd. It will make the texture a bit soft, which is not ideal for coating the cake, but great to use as a filling.

Makes enough to coat and fill a three-tier, 20cm (8in) cake

I will tell you a secret, this frosting is so delicious that sometimes I even use it as a cheesecake filling. It is smooth, spreadable, and easy to make and pipe decoratively. If you want to have a bit of tang, then replace half the amount of mascarpone with cream cheese and you will get the easiest cream cheese frosting.

Method

1   In a mixing bowl, whisk together the mascarpone and icing sugar using an electric whisk for 2–3 minutes.

2   Scrape down the sides of the bowl and add the double cream and vanilla. Whisk for few minutes more until you have a spreadable consistency.

DARK CHOCOLATE MASCARPONE FROSTING

Ingredients

250g (9oz) mascarpone
50g (1¾oz) cocoa powder, sifted
350ml (12fl oz) double (heavy) cream
1 teaspoon vanilla extract
100g (3½oz) dark chocolate,
  melted and cooled

Tip and variation

Take the mascarpone and cream out of the fridge about an hour before. If the mascarpone and cream is too cold, then melted chocolate will crystallise again and make this frosting speckled with chocolate instead of a smooth frosting.

✿ For white chocolate mascarpone frosting, replace the cocoa powder and dark chocolate with 150g (5½oz) white chocolate, melted and cooled.

Makes enough to coat and fill a three-tier, 20cm (8in) cake

This frosting is a great alternative to regular chocolate buttercream. It is smooth and not overly sweet. You can change the consistency of the frosting by adjusting the amount of cream.

Method

1   In a mixing bowl, whisk together the mascarpone and sifted cocoa powder using an electric whisk for 3–5 minutes until smooth.

2   Scrape down the sides of the bowl and add the double cream. Whisk for few minutes more to combine well, but take care not to over-whisk.

3   Finally, add the vanilla and cooled melted dark chocolate and whisk to combine.

CREAM CHEESE FROSTING

Ingredients

75g (2¾oz) unsalted butter,
  at room temperature
100g (3½oz) icing (confectioner's)
  sugar, sifted
150g (5½oz) full-fat cream cheese
  (take it out of the fridge about
  30 minutes before)
1 teaspoon vanilla bean paste

Variation

You can change the flavour of the
frosting by replacing the vanilla bean
paste with lemon, orange or almond
extract, or ground spices such
as cardamom or cinnamon.

Makes enough to coat and fill a two-tier, 20cm (8in) cake

This is one of the most delicious frostings ever. It has a tang from the cream cheese that makes it perfect to complement cakes such as carrot cake and red velvet cake. However, making a good cream cheese frosting can be tricky, and it often ends up with a soupy texture. To avoid this, make sure you use a full-fat cream cheese. Try not to use supermarket own brands or low-fat cream cheese, as these often don't contain enough fat to give your frosting the desired texture. Another important mistake to avoid is whisking the cream cheese for too long – if you over-whisk it, its texture tends to loosen and become soupy. Follow the method below and you should achieve the perfect cream cheese frosting.

Method

1   In a mixing bowl, whisk together the butter and sugar with an electric whisk for about 3–5 minutes until light and fluffy.

2   Scrape down the sides of the bowl and whisk for a further few minutes, then use a spatula to bring the butter and sugar mixture into the middle of the bowl.

3   Add the cream cheese and vanilla and whisk briefly for 30 seconds. Scrape down the sides of the bowl and whisk for another 30 seconds to fully combine. Once you've added the cream cheese, it's important not to whisk it too much.

4   This frosting can be kept in the fridge for up to one day. Take it out of the fridge and whisk really well for 30 seconds before using it.

DARK CHOCOLATE CREAM CHEESE FROSTING

Ingredients

150g (5½oz) full-fat cream cheese
(take it out of the fridge about an
hour before; if the cream cheese is
too cold the melted chocolate will
crystallise again)
70g (2½oz) salted butter,
at room temperature
1 teaspoon vanilla extract
200g (7oz) icing (confectioner's)
sugar, sifted
125g (4½oz) dark chocolate,
melted and cooled

Tip

Make sure the cream cheese is in the room
temperature while making the frosting.
If the frosting is cold as you add the melted
chocolate, the chocolate will start to
crystallise making the frosting looks
grainy and speckled.

Makes enough to coat and fill a two-tier, 20cm (8in) cake

This is my favourite chocolate frosting. The cream
cheese gives it a beautiful tang which complements the
sweetness of the chocolate very well. It is a great frosting
to fill, coat as well as pipe and decorate cakes.

Method

1   If there is any liquid on top of the cream cheese, place
the cream cheese on a muslin cloth to drain all the liquid.

2   In a mixing bowl, beat together the butter and vanilla using
an electric whisk for about 3 minutes until nice and fluffy

3   Scrape down the sides of the bowl, then the add cream cheese.
Whisk for about 30 seconds, then use a spatula to bring the
mixture into the middle of the bowl.

4   Add the sifted icing sugar in two stages, whisking for
30–45 seconds between each addition.

5   Finally, add the cooled melted chocolate and whisk for another
30 seconds to create a smooth and delicious chocolate cream
cheese frosting.

6   Best used immediately. However, if you want you can keep it in
the fridge for up to couple of days, then take it out and whisk
before using. Because of the amount of cream cheese, I would
prefer to use it all within few days.

CARAMEL CREAM CHEESE FROSTING

Ingredients

300g (11oz) full-fat cream cheese
175g (6oz) caramel sauce

Makes enough to coat and fill a two-tier, 20cm (8in) cake

This is one of the easiest yet the most delicious cream
cheese frosting of all. It complements chocolate
as well as coffee- and orange-flavoured cakes really well.

Method

1   Whisk the cream cheese using an electric whisk until spreadable.
Add the caramel sauce and whisk again for few minutes
till combined.

2   Scrape down the sides of the bowl and whisk for 20–30 seconds.

3   This frosting can be kept in the fridge for up to one day. Then
take it out of the fridge and whisk really well for 30 seconds
before using it.

Pastry crème

VANILLA PASTRY CRÈME

Ingredients

300ml (10½fl oz) whole (full-fat) milk
1½ teaspoons vanilla bean paste
4 large free-range egg yolks
50g (1¾oz) caster (superfine) sugar
30g (1oz) cornflour (cornstarch)
35g (1¼oz) cold salted butter, cubed

Variations

You can replace the vanilla with different flavouring elements to flavour your pastry.

✿ For lemon pastry crème, add the zest of 3 unwaxed lemons, along with ½ teaspoon vanilla bean paste.

✿ For orange pastry crème, add the zest of 1 large unwaxed orange and ½ teaspoon vanilla bean paste.

✿ For cardamom pastry crème, add 2 teaspoons ground cardamom and ½ teaspoon vanilla bean paste.

✿ For almond pastry crème, add 2 tablespoons amaretto and 1 teaspoon almond extract.

Makes enough to fill a three-tier, 20cm (8in) cake

This is a great alternative to buttercream to use as a filling. It is rich, creamy and velvety. Traditionally used for filling pastries like eclairs and millefeuilles, I like to use it to fill cakes too.

Method

1   Warm the milk and vanilla in a saucepan over a medium heat until just about to boil, but take it off the heat before it boils.

2   In a mixing bowl, whisk together the egg yolks, sugar and cornflour by hand until pale and fluffy.

3   Add the warm milk to the egg mixture and whisk thoroughly, with a balloon whisk then transfer the mixture back to the saucepan. Place over a medium heat andkeep whisking. As the mixture comes to the boil, it will begin to thicken. At this point, whisk it vigorously to create a smooth and shiny pastry crème.

4   Take the pan off the heat and add the cold cubed butter to the mixture, whisking continuously.

5   Pour into a heatproof bowl and cover with clingfilm, making sure the clingfilm touches the surface of the pastry crème; this will help prevent a skin from forming. Let it cool a little, then transfer to the fridge to cool completely.

6   Before using the pastry crème, remove it from the fridge and whisk to achieve a smooth, spreadable consistency.

7   This can be kept in the fridge for up to a couple of days. Take it out of the fridge before using and whisk until smooth.

FRUIT-FLAVOURED PASTRY CRÈME

Ingredients

300ml (10½fl oz) whole (full-fat) milk
½ teaspoon vanilla bean paste
6 large free-range egg yolks
50g (1¾oz) caster (superfine) sugar
60g (2oz) cornflour (cornstarch)
250g (9oz) fruit purée
60g (2¼oz) cold salted butter, cubed

Makes enough to fill a three-tier, 20cm (8in) cake

This is a slight variation on the vanilla pastry crème. The fruity flavours are achieved by incorporating some fruit purée. I like to use mango, raspberry, strawberry and passion fruit.

Method

1   Warm the milk and vanilla in a saucepan over a medium heat until just about to boil, but take it off the heat before it boils.

2   In a mixing bowl, whisk together the egg yolks, sugar and cornflour by hand until pale and fluffy.

Egg yolks start to thicken liquids at around 70–80°C (158–176°F). If the mix is heated above this temperature, it can cause the cream to curdle. That's why we add cornflour: it increases the thickening temperature to almost 100°C (212°F), giving us more time to work and reducing the chances of splitting the cream.

3 Add the warm milk to the egg mixture and whisk thoroughly, then transfer the mixture back to the saucepan. Place over a medium heat. Add the fruit purée and whisk using a balloon whisk. After 5–7 minutes, the mixture will start to thicken. Once this happens, reduce the heat to low and whisk vigorously to create a smooth, fruity pastry crème.

4 Take the pan off the heat and add the cold cubed butter to the mixture, whisking continuously.

5 Pour into a heatproof bowl and cover with clingfilm, making sure the clingfilm touches the surface of the pastry crème; this will help prevent a skin from forming. Let it cool a little, then transfer to the fridge to cool completely.

6 Before using the pastry crème, remove it from the fridge and whisk to achieve a smooth, spreadable consistency.

7 This can kept in the fridge for a couple of days. Whisk before using.

CRÈME DIPLOMAT

Ingredients

4 platinum-grade gelatine leaves
1 batch Vanilla Pastry Crème (page 40), prepared up to the end of step 4
300ml (10½fl oz) double (heavy) cream

Makes enough to fill a three-tier, 20cm (8in) cake

Crème diplomat is a version of set pastry crème mixed with whipped cream. It is a much lighter option and perfect for pairing with nut-based sponges.

Method

1 Soak the gelatine leaves in a bowl of cold water for 5–10 minutes. Squeeze out the excess water, then add to the hot pastry crème. Whisk thoroughly so that all of the gelatine dissolves.

2 Pour the mixture into a heatproof bowl and cover it with clingfilm, making sure the clingfilm is touching the surface of the pastry crème. Set aside to cool to room temperature.

3 Meanwhile, whip the double cream to soft peaks, then chill in the fridge.

4 Once the pastry crème has reach room temperature, whisk well until smooth. Fold in the cold whipped cream gently, adding it in two batches.

5 Use the crème diplomat immediately, as it will start to set quickly. Fill your cake, then leave it to set in the fridge for a couple of hours. As this recipe uses a significant amount of cream, it is best used immediately.

CRÈME MOUSSELINE

Ingredients

1 batch Vanilla Pastry Crème
(page 40), chilled
150g (5½oz) unsalted butter,
at room temperature

Tip

Ideally the pastry crème should at room
temperature before adding the butter,
otherwise, if it's too cold the butter might
start to crystallise in small particles,
making it look grainy.

Makes enough to fill and decorate a two-tier, 20cm (8in) cake

This crème mousseline is excellent for filling cakes
or piping on top.

Method

1   Remove the pastry crème from the fridge at least an hour
    before using and whisk using an electric whisk until smooth.
2   Whisk the butter separately until pale and fluffy using the
    same whisk.
3   Add the butter to the pastry crème a little at a time, whisking
    all the while. Once all the butter is incorporated, the mixture
    will have a much firmer yet lighter texture, and is ready to use.
    Use immediately.

CRÉMEUX

Ingredients

175g (6oz) white or dark
chocolate, chopped
1 batch Vanilla Pastry Crème
(page 40), or ½ batch Fruit-
flavoured Pastry Crème (page 40),
prepared up to the end of step 4

Makes enough to fill a three-tier, 20cm (8in) cake

Crémeux is pastry crème with added chocolate, and you
can use either dark or white chocolate depending on
your preference. If you like, you can make a fruit-based
chocolate crémeux by using fruit pastry crème instead
of vanilla pastry crème.

Method

1   Place the chopped chocolate in a heatproof bowl and pour
    the warm pastry crème over the top. Let it sit for few minutes
    to melt the chocolate, then whisk to combine.
2   Cover with clingfilm, ensuring the clingfilm is touching the
    surface of the crémeux, then and set aside until needed. You can
    this a day in advance if you like and keep it chilled in the fridge.
    Take it out of the fridge a couple of hours before you need it and
    whisk to get a spreadable consistency.

Bavarois

WHITE CHOCOLATE BAVAROIS

Ingredients

250ml (9fl oz) whole (full-fat) milk
100ml (3½fl oz) double (heavy) cream
1½ teaspoons vanilla bean paste
6 large free-range egg yolks
50g (1¾oz) caster (superfine) sugar
7 platinum-grade gelatine leaves
200g (7oz) white chocolate, chopped
400ml (14fl oz) whipping cream

Variation

You can make any fruit-based bavarois in the same way by replacing the milk with fruit purée. For example, for mango bavarois, replace the milk in the recipe with 250g (9oz) mango purée.

Makes enough to fill one 20cm (8in) mousse cake/imprimé

Bavarois is a type of lightened set custard. It makes a great creamy set filling for entremets or mousse cakes.

Method

1   In a small saucepan, warm the milk, double cream and vanilla over a medium heat until just about to boil. Take off the heat.

2   In a mixing bowl, whisk together the egg yolks and sugar by hand until pale and thick.

3   Pour the warm milk-and-cream mixture on top of the egg mixture and whisk to combine. Pour the mixture back into the saucepan and place over a medium heat. Stir continuously for 7–10 minutes as it starts to thicken, being very careful not to bring it to boil.

4   When the mixture is thick enough to coat the back of a spoon, take it off the heat.

5   Meanwhile, soak the gelatine leaves in cold water for 5–10 minutes, then squeeze out the excess water and add the leaves to the custard. Stir well to ensure the gelatine leaves are incorporated.

6   Place the white chocolate in a heatproof bowl and strain the custard through a sieve and into the bowl. Leave to sit for 5–10 minutes to let the chocolate melt, then whisk well to make a smooth white chocolate custard. Leave it to cool down a bit (preferably to room temperature).

7   Meanwhile, whisk the whipping cream in a large bowl until you have soft peaks.

8   When the white chocolate custard is almost at room temperature, start folding in the whipped cream, adding it in two or three stages.

9   Use the bavarois straightaway, and once you have filled your mousse cake or entremets, leave to set in the fridge for at least 3–4 hours or ideally overnight.

Caramel

CARAMEL SAUCE

Ingredients

200g (7oz) caster (superfine) sugar
75ml (5 tablespoons) water
200ml (7fl oz) double (double) cream
25g (1oz) salted butter

Tip

It is best to use a stainless-steel saucepan for making caramel, as you can see the change in colour more easily. If you use non-stick cookware, it is often difficult to identify the colour change.

Variations

✿ For vanilla caramel sauce, add 1 teaspoon vanilla extract after the cream is whisked in and the caramel is off the heat.

✿ For salted caramel sauce, add 1 teaspoon flaked of sea salt to the caramel and whisk it in when the caramel is ready and has been taken off the heat.

✿ For a ginger and salted caramel sauce, add 1 teaspoon flaked sea salt to the caramel and whisk it in. Add 1 teaspoon ground ginger while the sauce is still hot and whisk to combine. You could use 1 teaspoon ground cardamom instead.

✿ For peanut butter caramel sauce, add 100g (3½oz) smooth peanut butter (or chunky if you prefer texture) while the sauce is still hot, along with ½ teaspoon sea salt flakes, and mix well to combine.

✿ For miso caramel sauce, add 2–3 tablespoons miso paste while the sauce is still hot. The miso adds an amazing umami flavour to the caramel that takes it to the next level.

Makes enough to fill a three-tier, 20cm (8in) cake

Caramel sauce is great for using as drips as well as fillings for the cakes. It is all about the consistency and texture of the caramel when you use it. If you want to use it as a drip, let it cool to the room temperature on the worktop until it is runny but not hot. You can use this runny caramel for filling cakes or flavourings as well.

Method

1   In a deep stainless-steel saucepan, mix together the sugar and water. Place over a medium heat, and allow the sugar to caramelise. This will take 5–7 minutes. Do not stir the sugar anymore; you can swirl the pan from time to time if needed.

2   Meanwhile, in a separate saucepan over a medium heat, warm the cream until it is about to bubble.

3   Once the sugar starts to caramelise, give the pan a bit of swirl to ensure that all the sugar is caramelising evenly. To identify when the caramel is ready:

   ✿ Observe the colour: it will start to change from a straw colour to an amber brown.

   ✿ Listen to the sound: at the beginning, you will hear a lot of bubbling. However, as the sugar starts to caramelise, it will become much quieter.

   ✿ Pay attention to the smell: you should be able to detect the fragrance of caramel as the sugar caramelises. You need to be careful, though, as it takes only minutes for the sweet smell of caramel to transform into the bitter smell of burned sugar.

4   As the colour of the liquid changes to amber, take the caramel off the heat and add half of the warm cream. Whisk vigorously, but be careful as it happens, as the mixture has a tendency to sputter. Warming the cream beforehand should reduce this. Once it is incorporated, whisk in the remaining cream.

5   Finally, add the butter and whisk again. The butter gives a nice shine and smoothness to the final caramel sauce.

6   Pour the sauce into a heatproof bowl: this will help it cool faster. Cover with clingfilm, making sure the clingfilm touches the surface of the caramel to stop a skin from forming. The caramel needs to be cool or at room temperature before you use it, or it will melt the other filling/frostings.

FRUITY CARAMEL SAUCE

Ingredients

250g (9oz) caster (superfine) sugar
75ml (5 tablespoons) water
150ml (5½fl oz) double (heavy) cream
150g (5½oz) fruit purée
   (raspberry or passion fruit)
50g (1¾oz) salted butter

Makes enough to fill a three-tier, 20cm (8in) cake

This fruity caramel makes an exceptional addition to any cake. It can be used to add a bit of fruity flavour as well as tartness to your bakes. Raspberry and passion fruit are my favourite fruits to use here. If you've made your own fruit purée using a food processor, then pass it through a sieve before using it in this sauce.

Method

1   Make the caramel sauce as instructed on page 44, following the method from steps 1–4.

2   Once the cream is incorporated, whisk in the fruit purée. Once combined, add the butter and mix well.

3   Pour the sauce into a heatproof bowl and cover with clingfilm, making sure the clingfilm touches the surface of the caramel to stop a skin from forming. The caramel needs to be cool or at room temperature before you use it, or it will melt the other fillings or frostings. This can be kept in the fridge in an airtight container for a couple of days.

VEGAN COCONUT CARAMEL

Ingredients

200g (7oz) caster sugar
75ml (5 tablespoons) water
200g (7oz) coconut cream (see Note)
35g (1¼oz) coconut oil

Tip

To get coconut cream, store a can of full-fat coconut milk in the fridge overnight. The cream will separate from the watery liquid and rise to the top of the can. Open the can and carefully scoop the solid cream from the top.

Variation

Add 1 teaspoon ground cardamom or fennel seed when the caramel is taken off the heat to enhance its flavour.

Makes enough to fill a three-tier, 20cm (8in) cake

This particular caramel is one of my favourites. It brings back memories of Indian desserts filled with coconut and jaggery (a type of unrefined sugar).

Method

1   Follow the recipe for the caramel sauce on page 44, replacing the double cream with coconut cream and the butter with coconut oil. This can be kept in the fridge for a couple of days in an airtight container

WHIPPED CARAMEL

Ingredients

1 batch Salted Caramel Sauce
(Variations, page 44), chilled

Makes enough to fill and decorate a three-tier, 20cm (8in) cake

If you were to ask me 'What's better than caramel?', my answer would have to be whipped caramel. Whipping the caramel allows some air to be incorporated, making it much lighter in colour and texture. This provides an excellent filling for layer cakes and is also delicious spread over loaf cakes or traybakes. Before whipping, you will need to chill the caramel sauce in the fridge until it is almost solid – this will take about 3 hours.

Method

1   Take the Salted Caramel Sauce out of the fridge and whisk using an electric whisk for about 2 minutes. The colour of the caramel will lighten and the texture will become fluffy. This will lose its texture if you keep it too long, so it's best used immediately.

NUT BRITTLE

Ingredients

200g (7oz) caster (superfine) sugar
50ml (3 tablespoons) water
20g (¾oz) salted butter
100g (3½oz) toasted nuts or seeds

Makes enough to decorate a three-tier, 20cm (8in) cake

Nut brittle provides a great opportunity to add texture to your cake fillings. It can also be used as a decoration. You can use any nuts you like; I prefer hazelnuts, pecans, peanuts and pistachios. You can also use seeds, such as pumpkin, sunflower or sesame. Peanut and sesame brittle is my mum's favourite, and I always had it back in India, but I never knew it was so easy to make at home.

Method

1   Line a baking tray with baking paper or a silicone mat.

2   Combine the sugar and water in a deep, stainless-steel saucepan. Place over a medium heat. Don't stir the mixture once it's on the heat. Let the sugar start to caramelise.

3   It will take about 5–7 minutes for caramelisation to start (see page 44 for the signs to look out for). Once it does, swirl the pan carefully to ensure even heat distribution and caramelisation.

4   Once the caramel is a deep amber colour, add the butter and whisk well. Take it off the heat and add your nuts or seeds. Stir well to combine, then pour the mixture into the prepared tray. Spread it out so to form a single layer.

5   Leave to set and cool completely before using. To use this in a filling, you can chop it up into chunks. To use as a decoration, crack it into large or medium-sized shards. This can be kept in the fridge for about a week.

Ganache

DARK CHOCOLATE GANACHE

Ingredients

For filling a cake

200g (7oz) dark chocolate, chopped
200ml (7fl oz) double (heavy) cream
35g (1¼oz) salted butter

For chocolate drips or a quick chocolate glaze

100g (3½oz) dark chocolate, chopped
200ml (7fl oz) double (heavy) cream
35g (1¼oz) salted butter

For coating a cake

200g (7oz) dark chocolate, chopped
100ml (3½fl oz) double (heavy) cream
35g (1¼oz) salted butter

Tips and variations

Don't boil the cream, as soon as you see steam coming off the top of the cream, turn the heat off.

Chop the chocolate evenly so that all the chocolate melts at the same time.

For a flavoured ganache, you can infuse the cream with your choice of herbs, spices or citrus before adding to the chocolate.

✿ To make a herb-flavoured ganache, add 3 tablespoons freshly chopped mint or 4 tablespoons freshly chopped basil to the cream as you heat it. Once the cream comes close to the boil, take off the heat and leave to infuse for 15 minutes, then warm through once again and follow the rest of the method.

✿ To make a citrus ganache, add the zest of 2 medium oranges or 1 teaspoon orange extract to the cream as you warm it, then once it comes close to the boil, pour over the chopped chocolate and continue as above.

✿ To make a spiced ganache, add 2 teaspoons ground ginger or 2 teaspoons ground cardamom to the cream as you warm it, then once it comes close to the boil, pour over the chopped chocolate and continue as above.

Makes enough to fill, decorate or coat a two-tier, 20cm (8in) cake

You can't beat the velvety texture of a ganache. If I could, I would choose to cover and fill every cake I make with it. People often are a bit sceptical about preparing ganache, as they think it is too easy to split, but if you follow my recipe, hopefully yours will never split again. There are tips of how to salvage split ganache on page 26 as well. Similar proportions can be used to make a milk chocolate variation of ganache.

Method

1   Place the chopped chocolate in a heatproof bowl.

2   Warm the cream in a saucepan over a medium heat, taking care not to boil it. Pour the warm cream over the chocolate and leave to sit for 5 minutes.

3   Now add the butter and whisk until the chocolate has melted and everything is well combined. Cover with clingfilm, making sure the clingfilm is touching the surface of the ganache.

4   Always cool the ganache to room temperature before you use it. It will still be pourable at this stage. This consistency is perfect for drip or glazing. As you cool it further, it starts to thicken, which is what you need for filling and coating cakes.

5   If you place it in the fridge, it will chill and the texture becomes semi-solid – which is great to make truffles for decorative purposes. Also, at this stage if you want, you can whisk it to make a spreadable coating to use as a coating for cakes. It sets quickly making it easy to transport. Use straightaway or keep in the fridge for a few days.

WHIPPED DARK CHOCOLATE GANACHE

Ingredients

1 batch Dark Chocolate Ganache for
   Filling a Cake (page 49), chilled
or
1 batch Dark Chocolate Ganache for
   Coating a Cake (page 49), chilled

Makes enough to fill or coat a two-tier, 20cm (8in) cake

This whipped ganache can be used for filling cakes, but it's particularly good for covering them. It's easier to get a smoother finish with whipped ganache as it sets harder than regular ganache – and in addition, the greater the proportion of chocolate to cream in a ganache, the harder it sets. That's why whipped Dark Chocolate Ganache, which is two parts dark chocolate to one part double cream, is particularly good for coating tiered cakes, as it gives a strong and stable structure.

Before whipping, you need to chill the ganache in the fridge until it is semi-solid – this takes about 2 hours.

Method

1   Remove the ganache from the fridge and whisk for 30–45 seconds using an electric whisk until it becomes light and fluffy. As you whisk, it will become soft, spreadable and considerably lighter in colour. Use immediately.

GANACHE-BASED CHOCOLATE MOUSSE

Ingredients

3 platinum-grade gelatine leaves
150ml (5½fl oz) double (double)
   cream
200g (7oz) dark chocolate, chopped
300ml (10½fl oz) whipping cream

Makes enough to fill one 20cm (8in) entremet, mousse cake or imprimé

This chocolate mousse sets really well and gives a high-end patisserie look to sliced cakes. It tastes delicious when combined with nut-based sponges used in something like Charlotte russe.

Method

1   Soak the gelatine leaves in cold water for 5–10 minutes.
2   Meanwhile, warm the double cream in a saucepan over a medium heat until just about to boil, then take it off the heat.
3   Remove the gelatine leaves from the water and squeeze, then add them to the warm cream. Stir well to mix, ensuring the gelatine is fully dissolved.
4   Place the chocolate in a heatproof bowl and pour the warm cream over the top. Leave to sit for 5 minutes, then whisk well to combine. Set aside to cool to room temperature.
5   When you're ready, whisk the whipping cream in a bowl using an electric whisk until it holds soft peaks.
6   Gently fold the whipped cream into the cooled ganache, adding it in two stages. Once combined it is ready to be layered with your desired sponges. Keep in the fridge for 4–6 hours or preferably overnight, to set completely.

CARAMEL GANACHE

Ingredients

100g (3½oz) caster (superfine) sugar
50ml (2fl oz) water
100ml (3½fl oz) double (heavy) cream
25g (1oz) cold salted butter, cubed
75g (2¾oz) dark chocolate, chopped

Variation

To make a whipped caramel ganache,
chill the caramel ganache in the fridge
for a couple of hours until it is semi-solid,
then whisk using an electric whisk for
30–45 seconds, until it is much lighter
in colour and spreadable and smooth.

Makes enough to fill a two-tier, 20cm (8in) cake

This caramel ganache is great for filling a cake. It can also
be whipped (see Variation) to make a whipped caramel
ganache that is absolutely divine spread on top of a loaf
cake or traybake.

Method

1   In a saucepan, mix together the caster sugar and water.
    Place over a medium heat, but don't stir once it's on the heat.

2   After about 5–7 minutes, the sugar will start to caramelise
    (see page 44). Once this happens, you can swirl the pan
    to make sure the heat is getting distributed evenly.

3   Meanwhile, in a separate saucepan over a medium heat,
    warm the double cream until just about to boil.

4   Once the caramel becomes a deep amber colour, take it off
    the heat and add half of the warm double cream, whisking
    continuously. Add the rest of the cream and whisk until you
    have a smooth and glossy caramel.

5   Add the butter and whisk, then set aside for a few minutes.
    Ideally, you want the temperature of the caramel to come down
    to about 80–85°C (176–185°F). Once the caramel reaches the
    desired temperature, place the chocolate in a heatproof bowl
    and pour the caramel over the top. Leave to sit for 5–10 minutes,
    then stir it to combine.

6   Cover with clingfilm, ensuring the clingfilm touches the surface
    of the caramel ganache, and set aside until needed. It can be
    stored in the fridge for 2–3 days.

FRUIT-FLAVOURED GANACHE

Ingredients

200g (7oz) dark chocolate, chopped
120g (4¼oz) fruit purée
100ml (3½fl oz) whipping cream
    (this has a higher fat content than
    single cream, which stops it from
    curdling after adding fruit purée)
40g (1½oz) salted butter

Variations

✿ For a fruit ganache with a firmer texture, soak 2 platinum-grade gelatine leaves in cold water for 5–10 minutes. Remove from the water and squeeze, then whisk the gelatine leaves into the warm cream before pouring it on top of chocolate and fruit purée.

✿ For a boozy fruit ganache, add a few tablespoons fruit-flavoured alcohol and whisk in at the very end: for example, adding kirsch to a cherry ganache or raspberry liqueur to a raspberry ganache will give it an extra dimension.

Makes enough to fill a three-tier, 20cm (8in) cake

Adding a fruit purée to chocolate ganache gives it a fruity aroma and brings a tartness that really complements the richness of the chocolate. Fruits like strawberries, raspberries, passion fruit, blackberries, blackcurrants and cherries are particularly good here, as they pair extremely well with dark chocolate. However, you can experiment with any fruit purée you like. The consistency of this ganache is a little runnier than a normal ganache, but it's ideal for using as a cake filling.

Method

1   Place the chocolate and fruit purée in a heatproof bowl.

2   Heat the cream in a saucepan over a medium heat until it is about to boil.

3   Pour the warm cream over the chocolate and fruit purée and leave to sit for 5–10 minutes.

4   Add the butter and whisk until well combined, then cover with clingfilm, ensuring the clingfilm is touching the surface of the ganache.

5   This can be kept in the fridge for a couple of days, covered with clingfilm. Let it cool to the room temperature before using.

WHITE CHOCOLATE FRUIT GANACHE

Ingredients

300g (10½oz) white chocolate, chopped

75ml (2¾fl oz) double (heavy) cream

100g (3½oz) fruit purée, such as strawberry, raspberry, mango, passion fruit, blueberry or blackberry

Makes enough to fill a three-tier, 20cm (8in) cake

Fruit-flavoured white chocolate ganache makes an excellent cake filling, and can also be used as the base for a fruit-flavoured white chocolate mousse (using the same steps as for the Ganache-based Chocolate Mousse on page 50).

Method

1   Place the white chocolate and double cream in a microwave-safe bowl.

2   Microwave on high power in 30–second bursts, stirring in between, until all the chocolate is melted (around 1 minute to 1 minute 30 seconds in total).

3   Add the fruit purée and whisk to combine, then cover with clingfilm, ensuring the clingfilm is touching the surface of the ganache. Leave to cool to room temperature before use.

WHITE CHOCOLATE GANACHE FOR DRIPS

Ingredients

150ml (5½fl oz) double cream

1 teaspoon your chosen flavouring (such as vanilla bean paste, citrus extract, peppermint extract, or ground cinnamon, ginger or cardamom)

food colouring of your choice (optional)

100g (3½oz) white chocolate

Tip

Try to use an oil-based food colouring, which mixes with the ganache more uniformly.

Makes enough to decorate a two-tier, 20cm (8in) cake

When I started baking, I saw people making beautiful cakes with coloured drips. I knew how to do chocolate drips but wasn't sure how to make coloured drips. Then I discovered the trick, it is coloured white chocolate ganache. I am not sure how other bakers do it, but this is the way I do it and it works every time.

Method

1   Warm the double cream in a saucepan over an medium heat until it just starts to boil. Alternatively, pour it into a microwave-safe bowl and heat in the microwave on full power for 30–60 seconds until it just starts to boil.

2   Stir in your chosen flavouring and any colour you want to add.

3   Place the white chocolate in heatproof bowl and pour the warm cream over the top. Leave to sit for a few minutes, then whisk to combine.

4   Cover with clingfilm, making sure the clingfilm is touching the surface of the ganache to prevent it forming a skin. Leave to cool to room temperature before using.

5   It can be kept in the fridge for a couple of days, just make sure to warm it then let cool to room temperature before using.

WHITE CHOCOLATE GANACHE FOR FILLING AND COATING CAKES

Ingredients

300g (10½oz) white chocolate, chopped

100ml (3½fl oz) double (heavy) cream

1 teaspoon your chosen flavouring (such as vanilla bean paste, citrus extract, peppermint extract, or ground cinnamon, ginger or cardamom)

food colouring of your choice, if you are whipping the ganache, remember the colour will get considerably lighter, so adjust amounts accordingly (optional)

Variation

For whipped white chocolate ganache, prepare as above and then place the ganache in the fridge for a couple of hours until semi-set. It should be soft to the touch, but still have some resistance. Remove the clingfilm and whisk the ganache using an electric whisk for a few minutes. It will become very pale – almost white – and smooth and spreadable. This whipped ganache gives a smooth, crisp finish when filling and coating cakes.

Baking science

Due to the higher fat content of white chocolate, it is easy to accidentally split white chocolate ganache through overheating. The easiest way to resolve this is to add cold ingredients to the ganache. I normally start by adding about 40–50g (1½–1¾oz) chopped white chocolate to the split ganache. Whisk it in, then add 1 tablespoon cream and whisk again. Continue until your ganache returns to the desired smooth texture.

Makes enough to coat and fill a two-tier, 20cm (8in) cake

This ganache is exceptionally smooth and delicious, and sets brilliantly when whipped and used for frosting cakes. It's best to use the microwave method here as the cream and chocolate needs to be warmed and melted at the same time. If you don't have a microwave, you can use a bain-marie, with a heatproof bowl over boiling water.

Method

1   Place the white chocolate in a microwave-safe bowl and pour the double cream on top.

2   Microwave on full power in 30–second bursts, stirring between each one. It will probably take 1 minute to 1 minute 30 seconds in total to melt the white chocolate.

3   Add your chosen flavouring and whisk really well to combine, making sure there are no lumps of white chocolate left in the ganache.

4   Cover with clingfilm, making sure the clingfilm is touching the surface of the ganache. Leave to cool to room temperature.

5   You can use this as it is, but the true glory of this ganache is revealed when you whip it – see Variation. This can be kept in the fridge for couple of days. After that take it out of the fridge and allow it to reach room temperature. Let it get slightly soft before whipping it.

Fruit compote and jam

APPLE AND CINNAMON COMPOTE

Ingredients

2–3 cooking apples, chopped
2 tablespoons dark brown sugar
1½ teaspoons ground cinnamon
1 teaspoon vanilla bean paste
1 eating apple, chopped

Makes enough to fill a three-tier, 20cm (8in) cake

If you like apple pie, you will love this compote. A perfect filling for any apple cake. You can be experimental and use it to fill an autumnal ginger cake – it will work brilliantly with the warm flavours.

Method

1   Place the chopped cooking apples, brown sugar, cinnamon and vanilla in a saucepan over a low heat. Cover and cook for 5–10 minutes, or until the apples start to disintegrate.

2   Increase the heat to high and cook for a further 5 minutes, then take off the heat and add the chopped eating apple. Leave to cool to room temperature before use.

3   This can be kept in fridge for a couple of days.

PINEAPPLE AND PASSION FRUIT COMPOTE

Ingredients

400g (14oz) canned pineapple, drained and chopped
3 tablespoons caster (superfine) sugar
2 teaspoons grated fresh ginger
pulp of 3–4 passion fruits

Makes enough to fill a three-tier, 20cm (8in) cake

This is one of my favourite fruit compotes – it's full of tropical sunshine. It is not directly used to fill any cakes in the book but can be used to fill and sandwich coconut sponges or pineapple cake. You could even transform the strawberry and elderflower meringue cake to a pineapple and passion fruit meringue cake by stacking the meringue layers with freshly whipped cream and this compote.

Method

1   Place half the chopped pineapple in a saucepan with the caster sugar and ginger over a low–medium heat. Cook for 10 minutes until the pineapple disintegrates.

2   Take off the heat and add the rest of the pineapple, along with the passion fruit pulp. Set aside to cool completely.

3   This can be stored in a airtight container in the fridge for up to 3 days.

BLACKBERRY COMPOTE

Ingredients

300g (10½oz) blackberries,
   fresh or frozen
juice of 1 lemon
2 tablespoons caster (superfine)
   sugar
1½ teaspoons cornflour (cornstarch)
1 tablespoon water

Makes enough to fill a three-tier, 20cm (8in) cake

Every autumn I used to go for blackberry picking along the canal in Loughborough. Then in the evening into this compote and I used to drizzle some of this compote on top of my porridge in the morning. Later, I realised, this can be used as an excellent cake filling. Hence, I am sharing this recipe to enjoy a bit of autumn sunshine in your cake. PS: feel free to buy fresh or frozen blackberries if you are not into foraging.

Method

1   Place 200g (7oz) of the blackberries in a saucepan over a low heat, along with the lemon juice and sugar. Cover and cook for 10 minutes until the blackberries start to disintegrate.
2   In a cup or small bowl, mix together the cornflour and water, then stir this into the mixture in the saucepan. Keep stirring until the mixture starts to thicken. Add the rest of the blackberries and cook for 3–5 minutes so they are slightly cooked but still keep their texture.
3   Take off the heat and leave to cool before use.
4   This can be kept in the fridge in an airtight container for a couple of days.

FIG AND FENNEL COMPOTE

Ingredients

6 ripe figs
1 teaspoon ground fennel seeds
2 tablespoons caster sugar
zest and juice of 1 orange

Makes enough to fill a three-tier, 20cm (8in) cake

This compote combines the earthy fruitiness of figs with the anise flavour of fennel. It works great with any autumnal cake, like ginger cake or blackberry cake. Be creative, and don't hesitate to combine new flavours.

Method

1   Combine all the ingredients in a saucepan over a low–medium heat. Cook for 10–15 minutes until the figs start to disintegrate.
2   Take off the heat and set aside to cool completely before use.
3   This can be kept in the fridge in an airtight container for a couple of days.

BLUEBERRY AND LEMON COMPOTE

Ingredients

200g (7oz) blueberries,
    fresh or frozen
1 tablespoon caster (superfine) sugar
1 teaspoon ground cardamom
1 teaspoon ground ginger
zest and juice of 1 lemon
1 teaspoon cornflour (cornstarch)
1 tablespoon water

Makes enough to fill a three-tier, 20cm (8in) cake

Blueberry and lemon are a match made in heaven. But this compote has a little more: it has a bit of ginger with a hint of cardamom. This goes particularly well with my Lemon and Blueberry Cake on page 110, but is also delicious, with vanilla or lemon sponges.

Method

1   Place half the blueberries in a saucepan over a medium heat, along with the sugar, cardamom, ginger and lemon juice. Let it bubble away for 5–10 minutes. The berries will start to disintegrate. Take off the heat.

2   In a cup or small bowl, mix together the cornflour and water, then stir this into the mixture in the saucepan.

3   Return the saucepan to the heat and stir as the mixture thickens. Once it has a thicker consistency, take off the heat and add the rest of the blueberries. Mix well and set aside to cool. This can be kept in the fridge for a couple days in an airtight container.

CHERRY COMPOTE

Ingredients

200g (7oz) frozen stoned cherries
1 tablespoon caster sugar
1 teaspoon cornflour
1 tablespoon water

Makes enough to fill a three-tier, 20cm (8in) cake

This cherry compote is a must for any chocolate and cherry cake I make. I make this with frozen cherries, as these are available all the year around and are cheaper than fresh ones. However, if you have a cherry tree and have an abundance of cherries in late summer, please make this compote and freeze it in portions.

Method

1   Place 150g (5½oz) of the cherries in a saucepan over medium heat, along with the sugar. Cover and cook for 10 minutes until the cherries start to disintegrate.

2   Meanwhile, chop the remaining cherries and set aside.

3   After 10 minutes, mix together the cornflour and water in a small cup or bowl, then stir this into the mixture in the saucepan.

4   Keep stirring. As it starts to thicken, take the pan off the heat and stir in the chopped cherries. Leave to cool completely before using.

5   This can be kept in the fridge for a couple days in an airtight container.

MIXED BERRY JAM

Ingredients

250g (9oz) mixed berries
  (frozen or fresh)
200g (7oz) jam sugar
1 tablespoon lemon juice

Makes enough to fill a three-tier, 20cm (8in) cake

The main difference between jams and compotes is the amount of sugar. The amount of sugar in jams helps to preserve the fruit and its flavours longer. It does make it extremely sweet. Usually for jam the fruit to sugar ratio is 1:1, but I tend to decrease the amount of sugar to make the jam a bit tangier. Less sugar means difficulty in setting, but using jam sugar, which has added pectin in it, helps the jam to set even with less sugar. To be honest, if you are using it to fill cake, a runnier jam works perfectly fine.

Method

1   Place the berries in a medium-sized saucepan over a medium heat. Cover and leave to cook for 4–5 minutes until the fruit starts to break down.

2   Stir in the jam sugar and lemon juice and bring to the boil. Let the mixture boil for 5 minutes. If you have a jam thermometer, check the temperature of the jam. It should be between 105°C and 110°C (221–230°F).

3   As this jam will be used for cake fillings, it doesn't have to be as set as spreadable jam.

4   Once the jam is ready, pour it into sterilised jars and cover. Let it cool completely before using to fill a cake.

5   If you want to use the jam sooner, just spread it out in a baking tray to help it cool faster. It will keep in the fridge for up to 1 week.

STRAWBERRY JAM

Ingredients

250g (9oz) fresh strawberries, hulled
  and roughly chopped
170g (6oz) jam sugar
juice of ½ lemon

Variation

For a herb-infused strawberry jam, add 2–3 tablespoons chopped basil or tarragon.

Makes enough to fill a three-tier, 20cm (8in) cake

I love strawberry jam with chunks of strawberries in it. It adds a bit of texture in the filling, which shop-bought jam often lacks. It is so simple to make, and so rewarding.

Method

1   Place 200g (7oz) of the strawberries In a large saucepan over a medium heat. Add the sugar and cover, then bring to the boil. Once the mixture starts to boil, remove the lid.

2   Once the temperature of the jam reaches about 105°C (221°F), boil for a further 2–3 minutes, stirring occasionally to make sure that the jam does not stick to the bottom of the pan.

3   Take the pan off the heat and add the remaining strawberries, along with the lemon juice. Mix well. The jam will keep in a sterilised jar in the fridge for up to 1 week.

RASPBERRY JAM

Ingredients

250g (9oz) frozen raspberries
180g (6½oz) jam sugar
zest of 1 lemon

Variation

For a herb-infused raspberry jam, add 1 heaped tablespoon chopped thyme or lemon thyme at the end.

Makes enough to fill a three-tier, 20cm (8in) cake

Raspberries have got to be my favourite berries. Contrary to popular opinion I like seeded raspberry jam. The easiest way to make raspberry jam is to use frozen raspberries and jam sugar, and within 15-20 minutes your jam will be ready. By the time your cake is baked and cooled your jam is all prepared to be spread on the cake.

Method

1   Place 200g (7oz) of the raspberries in a large saucepan over a medium heat. Add the sugar and cover, then bring to the boil. Once the mixture starts to boil, remove the lid.

2   Once the temperature of the jam reaches about 105°C (221°F), boil for a further 2–3 minutes, stirring occasionally to make sure that the jam does not stick to the bottom of the pan.

3   Take the pan off the heat and add the remaining raspberries, along with the lemon zest. Mix well. The jam will keep in a sterilised jar in the fridge for up to 1 week.

PINEAPPLE, GINGER AND CHILLI JAM

Ingredients

200g (7oz) canned pineapple, drained and roughly chopped
2 tablespoons dark brown sugar
90g (3¼oz) jam sugar
2 teaspoons freshly chopped ginger
½ teaspoon chilli flakes

Makes enough to fill a three-tier, 20cm (8in) cake

This jam is my version of my mum's pineapple chutney. I think this is an excellent way to spice up your everyday cakes. The best part is if there is any leftover, you can have it with papadums, or even with a cracker!

Method

1   Place the pineapple, brown sugar and jam sugar in a saucepan over a medium heat and cook, covered, for 10–12 minutes.

2   Once the pineapple chunks have almost disintegrated, remove the lid and add the ginger and chilli and bring to the boil. Let the mixture boil for 5 minutes, but keep stirring to stop it sticking to the bottom of the pan.

3   Remove from the heat and let it cool before using to fill cakes. Or you can keep it in a sterilised jar in the fridge for up to a week.

Fillings and frostings

APRICOT JAM

Ingredients

500g (1lb 2oz) apricots, stoned and
   quartered
350g (12oz) jam sugar
2 teaspoons vanilla bean paste

Makes enough to fill a three-tier, 20cm (8in) cake

This apricot jam is a must if you are making a fruit cake. That little brushing of a good apricot jam over the top makes such a great difference. Also, if you have a jar handy, this jam is excellent for glazing fresh fruit decorations as well.

Method

1   Place the apricots and sugar in a stainless-steel saucepan and leave overnight to steep.
2   In the morning, place the pan over a medium heat and bring to the boil, stirring occasionally. Once boiling, stir in the vanilla bean paste, then let the mixture boil steadily for 5 minutes. Check the temperature with your sugar thermometer; it should be around 105.5°C (222°F).
3   Take off the heat and let the jam cool in the pan for 30 minutes.
4   If you are not going to use all of it to fill a cake, pour the rest into sterilised jars, while still warm. Seal and use within 2–3 weeks.

BLUEBERRY, LEMON AND CARDAMOM JAM

Ingredients

500g (1lb 2oz) frozen blueberries
zest of 3 lemons and juice of 2
350g (12oz) jam sugar
1 tablespoon ground cardamom

Makes enough to fill a three-tier, 20cm (8in) cake

You would not believe how good this is, until you try it yourself. This is very similar to the Blueberry Compote on page 58, but slightly sweeter. It is great not only for filling cakes, but also you can whisk it in with your Swiss and Italian meringue buttercream to get a blueberry buttercream.

Method

1   Place all the ingredients in a heavy-based saucepan over a medium heat and bring to the boil. Allow to boil for 5–10 minutes, stirring occasionally. Check the temperature with your sugar thermometer; it should be around 105.5°C (222°F).
2   Remove from the heat and leave to cool completely before you use it to fill cakes.
3   If you don't need to use all of the jam, pour the rest into sterilised jars while still warm. Seal and use within 2–3 weeks.

Curd

LEMON CURD

Ingredients

zest of 3 large lemons and juice of 2
3 large free-range egg yolks
100g (3½oz) caster sugar
Pinch of salt
60g (2¼oz) cold unsalted
   butter, diced

Variations

To make a lime curd, replace the lemon zest and juice with the zest of 7 limes and the juice of 5.

To make a fruit curd, replace the lemon zest and juice with 150g (5½oz) fruit purée, such as mango, passion fruit, strawberry or raspberry. Also half the amount of sugar to as fruits are inherently sweet.

Makes enough to fill one 20cm (8in) sandwich cake

In 2017, I took part in a baking competition in my friend David's church. My entry was a lemon cake filled with lemon curd. It was judged by Howard Middleton, a former *Bake Off* contestant. I asked him: 'How can I improve my cake?' He suggested that I make my own lemon curd, to make the difference! Since then, I am making my own – it is easy and so delicious compared to shop bought.

Method

1   Place all the ingredients except the butter in a saucepan and whisk until combined and smooth. Place over a medium heat, stirring continuously with a spatula. After 5–7 minutes, the mixture will start to thicken. Keep stirring until it is thick enough to coat the back of a spoon.

2   Now start adding the cubes of butter, one at a time, still stirring continuously. Once all the butter is incorporated, take the pan off the heat and leave to cool for 5–10 minutes.

3   Pour the curd into a sterilised jar to keep in the fridge for up to two weeks, or use it in your favourite cake or ice cream.

ORANGE AND CARDAMOM CURD

Ingredients

zest and juice of 3 oranges
6 large free-range egg yolks
120g (4¼oz) caster sugar
Pinch of salt
1½ teaspoons ground cardamom
90g (3¼oz) cold unsalted
   butter, diced

Makes enough to fill one 20cm (8in) sandwich cake

Once you learn how to make lemon curd, you can officially make any fruit and berry curd. Orange and cardamom is one of the variations which is excellent for filling any citrus, chocolate or caramel cake.

Method

1   Place all the ingredients except the butter in a saucepan and whisk until combined and smooth. Place over a medium heat, stirring continuously with a spatula. After 12–15 minutes, the mixture will start to thicken. Keep stirring until it is thick enough to coat the back of a spoon.

2   Now start adding the cubes of butter, one at a time, still stirring continuously. Once all the butter is incorporated, take the pan off the heat and leave to cool for 5–10 minutes.

3   Pour the curd into a sterilised jar to keep in the fridge for up to two weeks, or use it in your favourite cake or ice cream.

RASPBERRY AND YUZU CURD

Ingredients

200g (7oz) raspberry purée
50ml yuzu juice
75g (1¾oz) caster sugar
4 large free-range egg yolks
100g (3½oz) cold salted butter, diced

Variation

Replace the yuzu juice with an equal amount of lemon juice for raspberry and lemon curd.

Method

1   Place all the ingredients except the butter in a saucepan and whisk until combined and smooth. Place over a medium heat, stirring continuously with a spatula. After 5–7 minutes, the mixture will start to thicken. Keep stirring until it is thick enough to coat the back of a spoon.

2   Now start adding the cubes of butter, one at a time, still stirring continuously. Once all the butter is incorporated, take the pan off the heat and leave to cool for 5–10 minutes.

3   Pour the curd into a sterilised jar to keep in the fridge for up to a week, or use it in your favourite cake or ice cream.

2

DECOR AND ACCESSORIES

Marzipan

CLASSIC MARZIPAN

Ingredients

350g (12oz) whole blanched almonds
250g (9oz) icing (confectioner's)
  sugar
1–2 tablespoons amaretto
2 teaspoons almond extract

Variations

✿ For a citrus-flavoured marzipan, replace 1 teaspoon almond extract with 1 teaspoon lemon or orange zest or 1 teaspoon extract.

✿ If you don't want to use alchohol, replace the amaretto with 1 tablespoon golden syrup.

Makes enough to cover a three-tier 20cm (8in) cake

Please don't be shocked when I say that I never tasted marzipan before I came to the UK. The first time I had it, I was surprised to feel the almond explosion inside my mouth. I guess it was love at first bite. Marzipan has the reputation for being a covering for fruit cake but it can be used to layer and cover any cake, especially chocolate ones. Here is my recipe for homemade marzipan.

Method

1 In a food processor, blitz the blanched almonds to a fine powder.
2 Add the icing sugar, amaretto and almond extract and blitz on medium speed. The mixture will soon start to clump together.
3 Remove from the food processor and knead on a clean work surface dusted with icing sugar. If needed, you can add a few more drops of amaretto.
4 Cover the marzipan with clingfilm and set aside (at room temperature) until needed. It can be stored for about a week in the fridge.

PISTACHIO AND ROSE MARZIPAN

Ingredients

350g (12oz) shelled pistachios
250g (9oz) icing (confectioner's)
  sugar, plus extra for dusting
1–2 tablespoons rose water
1 teaspoon pistachio extract

Variation

For a boozy version, try swapping the rose water for with kirsch or raspberry liqueur; they both go really well with pistachio.

Makes enough to cover a three-tier 20cm (8in) cake

This marzipan is great to accompany citrus-based sponges – use it to coat lemon and raspberry cake. The citrus with the tartness of raspberry beautifully complements the pistachio and rose flavours.

Method

1 In a food processor, blitz the pistachios to a fine powder.
2 Add the icing sugar, rose water and pistachio extract and blitz on medium speed. The mixture will soon start to clump together.
3 Remove from the food processor and knead on a clean work surface dusted with icing sugar until smooth.
4 Cover the marzipan with clingfilm and set aside (at room temperature) until needed. It can be stored for about a week in the fridge.

HAZELNUT MARZIPAN

Ingredients

200g (7oz) whole blanched hazelnuts,
100g (3½oz) whole blanched
    almonds
250g (9oz) icing (confectioner's)
    sugar, plus extra for dusting
1–2 tablespoons hazelnut liqueur
1 teaspoon orange extract

Variation

If you are feeling experimental, you can swap in some plain caramel in place of the icing sugar – this will transform the marzipan into an absolutely delicious hazelnut praline variety.

Makes enough to cover a three-tier 20cm (8in) cake

If you ask what is my favourite marzipan, it will probably be this hazelnut one – I love the orange flavouring.

Method

1   Toast the hazelnuts in a dry frying pan over a medium heat for 5–7 minutes.

2   Transfer to a food processor, along with the almonds, and blitz to a fine powder.

3   Add the icing sugar, hazelnut liqeur and orange extract and blitz again. The mixture will soon start to clump together.

4   Remove from the food processor and knead on a clean work surface dusted with icing sugar until smooth.

5   Cover the marzipan with clingfilm and set aside (at room temperature) until needed. It can be stored for 3–4 days in the fridge.

MARZIPAN DECORATION AND MARZIPAN FLOWERS

Ingredients

1 batch Marzipan (page 67)
food colouring of your choice
icing sugar, for dusting

Makes enough to decorate a three-tier 20cm (8in) cake

Marzipan can not only be used for coating and covering, but it can also be used to make cake decorations and flowers. You can almost treat it as a fondant, but much tastier. In this book I mainly used decorations like flowers and leaves.

Method

To make flowers using plunger cutters

1   Take a walnut-sized piece of marzipan and add your desired food colouring. Dust the work surface with icing sugar and knead the marzipan to make it pliable and to work in the colour evenly.

2   Using a rolling pin and another dusting of icing sugar if needed, roll out the marzipan on a sheet of baking paper to a thickness of 4–5mm (¼in). Use a plunger cutter to cut out flower shapes. Transfer to a sheet of baking paper and keep covered until needed. Repeat to make as many as you need.

3   When you're ready to decorate your cake, you can use a palette knife to ease the flowers off the baking paper. Once positioned, roll small balls of marzipan and place them in the middle of each flower.

To make leaves using leaf cutters

4   Colour the remaining marzipan with green food colouring.
    Dust the work surface with icing sugar and knead the marzipan
    to make it pliable. Using a rolling pin and another dusting of
    icing sugar if needed, roll out the marzipan on a sheet of baking
    paper to a thickness of 3–4mm (⅛in). Use a leaf cutter to cut
    out leaf shapes.

5   If you like, you can score the leaves with the blunt edge of a knife
    to create the veins. Transfer to a sheet of baking paper and keep
    covered until needed.

Royal icing and honeycomb

ROYAL ICING

Ingredients

1 egg white
225–250g (8–9oz) icing
  (confectioner's) sugar, sifted
1 teaspoon lemon juice

Makes enough to decorate a two-tier 20cm (8in) cake

Royal icing was once the most popular medium for icing and decorating cakes, but in the past 50 years or so, it has fallen out of fashion, perhaps down to its excessive sweetness, with people favouring its delicious rivals: buttercreams and ganache.

I mostly use royal icing for decoration, celebrating its former glory by embossing it on top of modern buttercream or ganache frostings.

Method

1   In a mixing bowl, whisk together the egg white and one-third of the icing sugar using a balloon whisk until smooth. Add the lemon juice and half of the remaining icing sugar and whisk again.

2   Finally, whisk in the remaining icing sugar until the mixture is the thick consistency of royal icing: if you drag your finger through it, the gap left should remain for about 10 seconds.

3   Spoon the royal icing into a piping bag and set aside to be used later.

ROYAL ICING PANELS

Ingredients

1–1½ batches of Royal Icing
a few drops of your chosen
  food colouring

Tip

Pipe the panels the day before you will use them and leave to set overnight on the kitchen worktop. The trick is to get it dried completely.

Makes enough to decorate a two-tier 20cm (8in) cake

My most favourite way of decorating cakes is with royal icing panels. It might be a bit fiddly but so rewarding that you would like to do it again. Traditionally the patterns inside the panelling is geometric, but I usually let my imagination flow freely and fill the panel with royal icing swirls. Hope you will enjoy making them as much as I do.

Method

1   Measure the sides of the cake that you want to cover with royal icing panels. For the pattern, you can either print a rectangular template (adjusting the dimensions to fit your cake) or make your own, drawing it onto a piece of A4 paper or directly onto baking paper. Place
a sheet of baking paper over the printed or drawn A4 sheet and clip together. If you have drawn the template directly on to baking paper, simply turn it over so the pencil side is facing down.

2   Carefully pipe the royal icing, following the template. Repeat three more times, until you have enough icing panels to cover all four sides of the cake.

3   If you wish, you may also use some of the royal icing to pipe some decorations, or to create a cake topper or some hanging filigree shapes. Leave all the panels and decorations to dry completely, preferably overnight.

4   Once they are completely dry, carefully peel off the baking paper.

5   Use buttercream or some more royal icing to attach it the panels to the sides of the cake. Pipe over or otherwise decorate the joins between the panels to hide them.

6   For coloured panels, divide the remaining royal icing between 2–3 bowls and mix with different food colouring. Spoon into separate piping bags and pipe the coloured royal icing on to the panels to create a colourful pattern.

HONEYCOMB

Ingredients

butter, for greasing
100g (3½oz) caster (confectioner's) sugar
90g (3¼oz) golden syrup
1½ teaspoons bicarbonate of soda

Tips

You can flavour the honeycomb by adding 1 teaspoon different spices and flavourings. My personal favourites are ground ginger, vanilla extract and dried thyme.

Make sure you have all the ingredients weighed out and ready before you begin. This is a very speedy process and you need to act quickly.

Makes 10–15 medium-sized pieces

Honeycomb/cinder toffee is the ultimate kitchen science experiment. Please use caution as you are dealing with sugar between 150°C and 160°C (300–320°F). Do remember to wait until it has completely cooled before you crack it. Making the first crack is super satisfying. Honeycomb is not only great as a cake topper, but is equally delicious crumbled over some ice cream.

Method

1   Grease a baking tray and line with baking paper.

2   In a large saucepan, mix together the sugar and golden syrup with a metal spoon. Place over a medium heat and let the sugar melt. Don't stir the mixture, but you can swirl the pan from time to time to ensure the sugar melts evenly.

3   Keep checking the temperature of the sugar mixture using a sugar thermometer. When the temperature reaches 150°C (302°F), known as 'hard-crack temperature', take the pan off the heat and add the bicarbonate of soda. Mix well. Be very careful, as the mixture might splatter at this point.

4   Pour the honeycomb mixture on to the prepared baking tray, then leave for 30 minutes to set and cool.

5   Once cooled, break the honeycomb into shards and use it to decorate your cakes.

Chocolate

TEMPERING CHOCOLATE

Ingredient

300g (10½oz) dark or white chocolate, chopped

Makes enough to decorate two two-tier 20cm (8in) cakes

If you want to make chocolate decorations, you need to know how to temper chocolate. This is what gives chocolate its shine and snap – it is like the password to the chocolate sculpture world. Once you know that secret, you can transform your prettiest dreams into chocolate masterpieces.

Method

To temper dark chocolate

1   Place two-thirds of the dark chocolate in a heatproof bowl set over a saucepan of simmering water and melt. You want the temperature to reach about 48°C (118°F). Alternatively, you can place the chocolate in a microwave-safe bowl and melt in a microwave on full power in 30–second bursts, stirring between each one. Be very careful when melting chocolate in the microwave, as it is easy to burn it!

2   Once the chocolate has reached 48°C (118°F), take it off the heat and add the remaining third. Mix well.

3   Now you want the temperature of the chocolate to come down to 28°C (82°F). Adding the unmelted chocolate will help with this. The added tempered chocolate will also encourage the growth of tempered chocolate crystals in the melted chocolate. You can either leave the chocolate on the side to cool, stirring from time to time, or you can place the bowl of melted chocolate in a larger bowl filled with iced water to cool it faster.

4   Once the temperature reaches 28°C (82°F), it's time to heat the chocolate once more, either over the pan of simmering water or in the microwave, until it reaches about 32°C (90°F).

5   The chocolate is now tempered and ready to use. Keep the temperature of the chocolate at about 32°C (90°F). If it falls below 28°C (82°F) while you are making your decorations, just reheat it to 32°C (90°F).

To temper white chocolate

6   The process for tempering white chocolate is exactly same as above, but the temperatures are different because white chocolate has a higher fat content and lower melting point. So for white chocolate, melt it and heat to 45°C (113°F), then cool to 27°C (81°F), before reheating to 29°C (84°F).

Chocolate decorations

CHOCOLATE SHARDS

1   Line a baking sheet with baking paper or acetate.

2   Spoon around 70g (2½oz) of tempered dark chocolate on to the baking paper or acetate and spread it out using a palette knife.

3   Place in the fridge for a few minutes until the chocolate just starts to set, then remove from the fridge and score the chocolate into shard shapes using the tip of a palette knife. Return to the fridge to set completely.

4   Once set, remove from the fridge and carefully peel the shards from the baking paper or acetate. They should separate automatically, but if not you can press lightly along the score lines to encourage the shards to separate.

DOUBLE CHOCOLATE SHARDS

1   Line a baking sheet with baking paper or acetate.

2   Drizzle a few tablespoons of tempered white chocolate over the baking paper or acetate. If you prefer, you can pipe some designs with the white chocolate instead of just drizzling. Place in the fridge for couple of minutes to set.

3   Next, pour 70g (2½oz) of tempered dark chocolate on top and spread out using a palette knife.

4   Place in the fridge for a few minutes until the chocolate just starts to set, then remove from the fridge and score the chocolate into shard shapes using the tip of a palette knife. Return to the fridge to set completely.

5   Once set, remove from the baking paper or acetate as explained above.

CHOCOLATE SAIL

1   Fold a 30 × 30cm (12 × 12in) piece of baking paper like a fan and then flatten it. Place on a baking sheet.

2   Spread 100g (3½oz) of tempered dark or white chocolate over the baking paper with a palette knife. Place in the fridge about 30 seconds until it starts to set, but make sure it does not yet set completely, as you need to shape the sail.

3   Remove from the fridge and fold the baking paper using the folding marks on the baking paper. Secure using pegs and return to the fridge to set.

4   Once set, remove from the fridge and remove the pegs. Carefully unmould the sail from the baking paper. Return to the fridge until needed.

DOUBLE CHOCOLATE COLLAR

1   Measure the perimeter of your cake using a piece of string to determine the length of the chocolate collar you will need. Cut an acetate strip or baking paper to your desired length.

2   Fill a piping bag with 150-200g (5½–7oz) tempered white chocolate and pipe designs on the acetate strip. If the chocolate is properly tempered, it will start to set within a few minutes.

3   Once the white chocolate is almost set, spoon 300g (10½oz) tempered dark chocolate over the top. Spread the dark chocolate over the acetate strip using a palette knife.

4   Leave for a couple of minutes to allow the dark chocolate to partially set, then quickly but carefully lift up your acetate strip and wrap it around the cake, with the chocolate side touching the cake. Place the cake in the fridge and let the collar set for 15–20 minutes.

5   Once set, remove from the fridge and carefully remove the acetate strip, revealing the perfectly shiny chocolate collar underneath.

CHOCOLATE CURLS

1 Take an A4 acetate sheet or a baking paper with similar size. Pour the tempered chocolate on of the baking paper. Spread the chocolate evenly using a palette knife.

2 Let the chocolate set for 5 minutes. Then use the blunt side of a knife to score the chocolate.

3 Now, roll the acetate carefully and place between two chef's rings/cookie cutter so it forms a cylinder. Place it in the fridge for 30 minutes to set completely.

4 Once set, take it out of the fridge and carefully unroll the acetate. As you unroll the acetate, the curls should start to separate automatically.

5 You can also make a chocolate curl in a leaf shape. To do that, spread about 50–75g (1¾–2½oz) tempered chocolate on acetate. Take a comb for chocolate decoration and drag lines of chocolate on the tempered chocolate.

6 To make it resemble like leaf, you can drag the lines away from an imaginative center line on both side of the line.

7 Use your finger to draw a leaf shape around the border of the chocolate. Now roll the acetate and place between two cookie cutters or chef's ring so it forms a cylinder. Place in the fridge to set for 30 minutes.

8 Once set, take it out of the fridge and unroll carefully. The leaf should separate easily from the acetate.

9 Keep the curls and the leaf in the fridge until it needs to be used.

CHOCOLATE DOME

1 Spoon 200g (7oz) tempered dark chocolate into a piping bag.

2 Place a full balloon on top of a chef's ring or on top a bowl and set this on a plate or tray. Dip a kitchen towel in little vegetable oil and rub all over the balloon.

3 Snip the end of the piping bag and drizzle the chocolate in circles all over the balloon (see photo overleaf). Chill in the fridge for 10–15 minutes, then take it out of the fridge and pipe another set of little circles all over the balloon. Return to the fridge for 30 minutes to set completely.

4 Once set, remove the chocolate-covered balloon from the fridge. With sharp scissors, make an incision in the balloon and, once deflated, carefully remove the balloon from the chocolate dome.

5 Place the chocolate sphere on a baking sheet lined with baking paper and return to the fridge to chill.

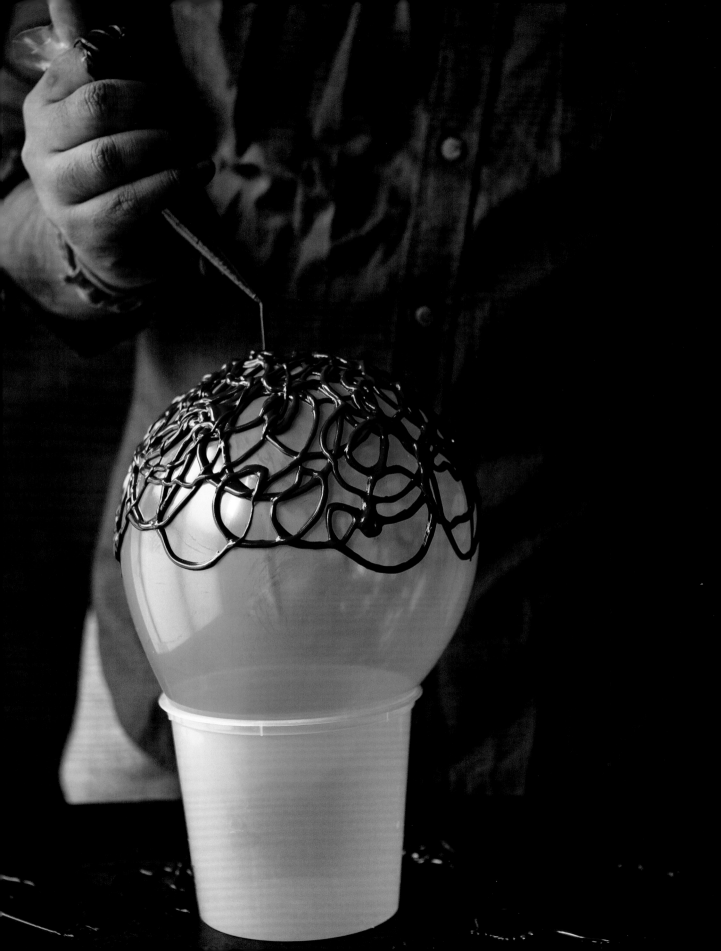

CHOCOLATE FLOWER

Ingredient

100-150g (3½-5½oz)
   tempered chocolate

Makes enough for the flower shown, opposite

The first time I saw a chocolate flower was in the 2017 series of *Bake Off*, where Sophie Faldo made one to decorate her final entremets. It was so beautiful that I wanted to try it myself. Mine is not as pretty as hers but does the job, and here is how I make it.

Method

1 Spoon the tempered chocolate into a piping bag.

2 Cut a couple of 5-7cm (2-2¾in)-wide and 15-25cm (6-10in)-long strips of acetate or baking paper. If you have ia kitchen roll tube, that will be handy to shape the petals. Cut the tube lengthways so you have two long curved sections of cardboard.

3 Snip the end of the piping bag to create a 5mm (¼in) opening. Pipe 10–12 blobs of chocolate about the size of a coin on the acetate/baking paper strip, spacing them about 1cm (½in) from each other and from the edge. Use the blunt end of a table knife to drag a little bit of the chocolate to the edge of the strip.

4 Now hold the sides of the strip and shake it vertically, so that the chocolate starts to drop and create a petal shape. Then slide the strip inside the curved cardboard and place it in the fridge to set.

5 Once the chocolate is set, you can start the construction of the flower. If you have a freezer spray, it will be very handy for this stage.

6 Take a 5 × 5cm (2 × 2in) piece of baking paper and place on a flat surface. Pipe a 1cm (½in) circle of tempered chocolate in the middle of the paper.

7 Carefully peel the petals away from the strip of acetate or baking paper. They will be slightly curved. Arrange about 6 to 8 petals on top of the tempered chocolate circle.

8 If you have the freezer spray, spray it on top so the chocolate petals stick to the base. Otherwise transfer to the fridge for 5–10 minutes to set.

9 Once set take it out of the fridge. Pipe some more tempered chocolate in the middle of the flower. Arrange another 6 petals in the middle. Use the freezer spray to make it set, or transfer it to the fridge for a further 10 minutes. You can repeat this step to add another 6 petals if you want.

10 Once you are happy with how the flower looks, pipe little beads of tempered chocolate in the middle to resemble stamens and the stigma of a flower. Keep it in the fridge until you need to use it to decorate.

Decor and accessories

Buttercream flowers and decorations

Ingredients

½ batch of Swiss Meringue
  Buttercream (page 34)
food colouring
brown sprinkles (optional)

Tip

Using a piping nozzle coupler
provides a great advantage over
inserting the piping nozzle directly
into the piping bag, as it allows you
the flexibility of switching between
different piping nozzles for the same
piping bag.

Makes enough to decorate a two-tier 20cm (8in) cake

To make buttercream daisies

This is the easiest of the buttercream flowers. For daisy petals,
you will need a petal nozzle. For the centre of the daisies, you can
use a 1–2mm (⅛in) piping nozzle, but I tend to simply cut the end
of the piping bag to create a 1–2mm (¹⁄₁₆in) opening.

1   Transfer 2–3 tablespoons of the buttercream into a separate
    bowl and use yellow food colouring to colour it yellow, leaving
    the rest white.
2   Spoon the white buttercream into a piping bag fitted with
    a piping nozzle coupler. Attach your chosen petal-piping
    nozzle using the coupler.
3   Fill a second piping bag with the yellow buttercream.
4   Take a 5cm (2in) square of baking paper and place it on top of
    a flower icing nail. Secure it in place with a little bit of buttercream.
5   Hold the piping bag at a 45-degree angle, and hold the flower
    nail in your other hand. Starting about 5mm (¼in) away from
    the edge of the baking paper, and with the wide end of the tip
    pointed outwards, apply pressure and pull the piping bag
    towards the centre of the flower nail, releasing the pressure
    to complete the petal. Repeat, leaving about 2–3mm (¹⁄₁₆–⅛in)
    between each petal and rotating the flower icing nail as you go
    until you have about 10–12 petals and have formed a complete
    circle. Now, pipe little dots of yellow buttercream in the centre
    in a cluster to create the centre of the daisy.
6   Once the flower is complete, carefully lift the baking paper
    holding the flower off the flower nail and place on a baking tray.
7   Repeat to make as many daisies as you wish. When all are
    transferred to the baking sheet, place them in the freezer
    for 30–40 minutes to set completely.
8   Once set, peel them away from the baking paper and carefully
    place on the cake to decorate.

To make buttercream sunflowers

Sunflowers are another simple flower to make using buttercream.
For sunflowers, you will need a leaf nozzle. For the inside of the
sunflowers, you will need a 2–3mm (¹⁄₁₆–⅛in) nozzle.

1   Transfer two-thirds of the buttercream into a separate bowl
    and use yellow food colouring to colour it yellow. Colour the
    remaining third with brown or black food colouring.
2   Spoon the yellow buttercream into a piping bag fitted with
    a piping nozzle coupler. Attach your chosen leaf nozzle using
    the coupler.

3   Spoon the brown or black buttercream into a separate piping bag fitted with a 2–3mm (⅟₁₆–⅛in) nozzle.

4   Take a 5cm (2in) square of baking paper and place it on top of a flower icing nail. Secure it in place with a little bit of buttercream.

5   Holding the flower nail in one hand and the piping bag in the other, pipe a 2½cm (1in) circle of brown or black buttercream in the middle of the baking paper.

6   Now switch to the piping bag with the leaf nozzle. Position the nozzle at a 20-degree angle, touching the edge of the brown circle. Squeeze the piping bag until it pipes a wide base of yellow buttercream, then gently pull away, slowly reducing the pressure on the bag.

7   When you are satisfied with the length of the petal, stop squeezing the piping bag and pull quickly to complete the petal.

8   Repeat the process to pipe one set of petals around the circle, rotating the flower nail as you go. Next, pipe another layer of petals on top in the same way, but this time at a steeper angle of 30–35 degrees. Make sure the base of the second layer of petals is just next to the first layer so that their bases are touching.

9   Finally, pipe a cluster of brown or black dots inside the circle to create the centre of the sunflower. You can add some brown sprinkles to give extra detail.

10 Once the sunflower is complete, carefully lift the baking paper holding the flower off the flower nail and place on a baking tray.

11 Repeat to make as many sunflowers as you wish. Once all are transferred to the baking sheet, place them in the freezer for 30–40 minutes to set completely. Once set, peel them away from the baking paper and carefully place on the cake to decorate.

To make buttercream chrysanthemums

I personally love chrysanthemums, and they are simple and straightforward to pipe. You will need a 'chrysanthemum nozzle' such as the Wilton 81. You will also need a 2–3mm (⅟₁₆–⅛in) piping nozzle, or if you prefer you can just snip a 2–3mm (⅟₁₆–⅛in) opening in your piping bag.

1   Transfer a couple of tablespoons of the buttercream to a separate bowl and colour it with yellow food colouring for the stamens. Chrysanthemum petals can be any colour, so it's up to you to choose which colour you want to dye your remaining buttercream. You can keep it white if you wish; white chrysanthemums look gorgeous too.

2   Fill a piping bag fitted with a chrysanthemum nozzle with the buttercream of your chosen colour. Spoon the yellow buttercream into a separate piping bag fitted with a 2–3mm (⅟₁₆–⅛in) nozzle, or snip a 2–3mm (⅟₁₆–⅛in) opening in the end.

3   Take a 6 (2½in) square of baking paper and place it on top of a flower icing nail. Secure it in place with a little bit of buttercream.

4   Holding the flower icing nail in one hand and the piping bag in the other, pipe a 4cm (1½in) circle of yellow buttercream in the middle of the baking paper.

5   Now switch to the other piping bag. Position the chrysanthemum nozzle at a 25–30-degree angle, with the curved end downwards and touching the yellow circle. Gently squeeze the piping bag as you slowly pull it away from the centre. Once you are happy with the length, stop squeezing and pull the piping bag abruptly to end the petal. Repeat until you have a full set of petals around the circle, rotating the flower icing nail as you work.

6   Repeat this process to pipe a few more layers of petals on top, increasing the angle each time and making sure each layer starts where the previous layer finishes. The length of the inner petals should gradually become shorter than that of the outer petals.

7   Use the yellow buttercream to pipe some short spikes in the centre to represent the stamens of the flower.

8   Once the chrysanthemum is complete, carefully lift the baking paper holding the flower off the flower icing nail and place on a baking tray.

9   Repeat to make as many chrysanthemums as you wish. When all are transferred to the baking sheet, place them in the freezer for 1 hour to set completely. Once set, peel them away from the baking paper and carefully place on the cake to decorate.

To make buttercream roses

Roses are little more complicated to make, but very satisfying. You can even flavour the buttercream with rose water to make it extra realistic. You'll need a petal nozzle for the rose petals (any kind will do), and a separate piping bag with a 1cm (½in) opening for the rose bases. Colour the buttercream with the colour of your choice (you may choose to make two- or three-tone roses), then divide it between the piping bag fitted with the petal nozzle and a separate piping bag with a 1cm (½in) opening cut in the end.

1   Take a 6 (2½in) square of baking paper and place it on top of a flower icing nail. Secure it in place with a little bit of buttercream.

2   In the middle of the baking paper, pipe a mound of buttercream about 1–1½cm (½–¾in) high using the piping bag with the 1cm (½in) opening.

3   Now switch to the piping bag with the petal nozzle. Hold the nozzle vertically, tilting it slightly inwards. Make sure the wide end of the nozzle is touching the surface of the mound. Squeeze the piping bag as you turn the flower nail until both ends meet. This will create the inside bud of the rose.

4   Keeping the nozzle in the same position, suntil tilting inwards, pipe an arch-shaped petal that goes around the bud. Make sure there is no gap between the first petal and bud. Repeat to create 2–3 more petals around the bud. Each petal should start slightly past the middle of the previous petal and overlap it.

5   Next, reposition the nozzle so it's straight, and pipe another 3–4 petals that are slightly longer and taller than the inside petals.

6   Finally, tilt the nozzle slightly outwards and pipe another 3–4 petals, this time slightly longer than the previous ones but not higher.

7   Once the rose is complete, carefully lift the baking paper holding the flower off the flower icing nail and place on a baking tray.

8   Repeat to make as many roses as you wish. Once all are transferred to the baking sheet, place them in the freezer for 1 hour to set completely. Once set, peel them away from the baking paper and carefully place on the cake to decorate.

To make buttercream foliage

Just as any flower arrangement is incomplete without foliage, any buttercream flowers need some buttercream leaves to finish the look I tend to pipe the foliage and leaves straight on to the cake after the flowers have been positioned. Keep a few leaf nozzles on hand and with your colours, using different shades of green.

1   Divide your buttercream between a few bowls and colour them in your chosen shades of green, then spoon the green buttercreams into piping bags fitted with leaf nozzles. To make variegated leaves, spoon a darker shade of green into a piping bag fitted with a leaf nozzle and spread it around the sides of the bag, then spoon a lighter or yellower shade of green into the middle of the bag.

2   Hold the piping bag and leaf nozzle vertically, next to the surface on to which you want to pipe the leaves. Squeeze the piping bag gently, and once you get the desired length of leaf, pull abruptly to finish.

3   You can change the direction of the leaves by tilting the nozzle inwards and outwards. Repeat this technique as necessary to decorate.

4   After you've finished piping the leaves, chill the cake in the fridge for a few hours to give the leaves time to set.

SUGAR PASTE FLOWERS

Ingredients

100g (3½oz) sugar paste
1 teaspoon vegetable shortening
  (if needed)
food colouring of your
  choice (optional)
cornflour, for dusting
edible gold dusting
Royal Icing (page 70)
edible gold paint (optional)

Makes 3–4 flowers

Sugar paste is an excellent tool for crafting flowers for cake decorating. It has been used for years and is an artform in its own right. It's possible to use sugar paste to create elaborate flowers that are beautiful to look at, but they require a certain set of tools that are not always easily available in a home baker's kitchen. This flower is very simple, and can be made without any special tools. You'll just need a set of petal cutters, a rolling pin, a tablespoon and a few paper cupcake cases. You can colour the sugar paste with food colouring if you wish, but I like to keep it white and then paint the edges of the petals with edible gold paint.

Method

1   The first step of working with sugar paste is to knead it well. If you feel it is sticking to your hands, use the tiniest amount of vegetable shortening to grease your hands slightly, then continue to knead until soft and pliable. If you want to colour the sugar paste, add the food colouring as you knead.

2   Dust the work surface with cornflour and use a rolling pin to roll out the sugar paste to a thickness of 2–3mm (¹⁄₁₆–⅛in): the thinner, the better, as this will help the flower petals dry faster.

3   Use the petal cutter to cut out some petal shapes. I tend to use the cutters with five petals.

4   Once cut, place the petals on a sponge pad. Use the back of a spoon to press the edges of the petals, making them even thinner. Once you're happy with them, arrange the petals inside a paper cupcake case to give you a flower shape. Repeat to make as many flowers as you want, remembering to reserve some of the paste for the insides of the flowers. For the insides, take a peanut-sized piece of sugar paste and roll it between your palms to make a smooth ball. Repeat to make one for each flower, then leave the petals and sugar-paste balls to dry overnight. Once dry, toss the balls in edible gold dust. Carefully place one in the middle of each flower and secure using royal icing. Leave for a few hours for the royal icing to set.

5   Use the flowers to decorate your cakes. If you like, you can paint the edges of the petals gold for an elegant look.

WAFER PAPER SAILS

Ingredients

boiling water

A4 sheet of wafer paper,
   halved lengthways

food colouring of your choice,
   diluted with vegetable oil
   or vodka (optional)

Variation

To make other wafer paper shapes,
simply steam the paper as above
and fold into your desired shape.

Makes one sail

Wafer paper is made with potato starch and can be used to create striking decorations. I have used this technique numerous times to creative impressive fan-shaped paper 'sails' for my cakes. They give a gorgeous, eye-catching look with minimal effort.

It's important to remember that wafer paper tends to dissolve when in touch with water, but you do need a bit of moisture to be able to shape it, so I tend to steam my wafer paper before shaping. When painting or colouring wafer paper, it is better to use petal dust. If you are using gel food colouring, remember to dilute the colour with oil or alcohol to minimise the risk of the paper dissolving. This edible 'paper' doesn't have any flavour on its own, but if you want, you can always brush it with a bit of flavouring mixed with alcohol.

Method

1   Carefully pour the boiling water into a shallow bowl. Hold the paper over the bowl, in the steam.

2   As the paper comes into contact with the steam, it gets more pliable. Move the paper around slowly to make sure it gets evenly exposed to the steam.

3   Once all the paper has been 'steamed', you can start to fold it. Fold the paper backwards and forwards in thin strips until it resembles a Chinese fan. Dampen your fingers slightly and use them to 'glue' the ends of the wafer paper sail together. Leave to dry completely.

4   If you want, you can paint the fan with food colouring diluted with vegetable oil or vodka.

WHITE MODELLING CHOCOLATE

Ingredients

200g (7oz) white chocolate
55g (2oz) golden syrup

Tips

To make coloured modelling chocolate, add a few drops of oil-soluble colours in the melted white chocolate. Mix well and then add the golden syrup.

To make dark modelling chocolate, use 200g (7oz) dark chocolate and 100g (3½oz) golden syrup.

If during kneading it starts to become too oily, stop kneading. Wrap in clingfilm and place in the fridge for a couple of hours.

Makes enough to decorate a two-tier 20cm (8in) cake

Modelling chocolate is great for making cake decorations. Whether it is flowers, sculpture or figurines, everything can be made easily using modelling chocolate. You can treat it almost like a playdough. After shaping the decorations, you need to place them in the fridge for 2–3 hours or in the freezer for an hour to set. Use them as needed.

Method

1   Melt the chocolate in a microwave in full power in 30–second bursts. Stir between each burst to make sure all the chocolate is melted.

2   Once melted, mix the golden syrup with the melted chocolate. Mix until there no streaks of golden syrup are visible. Be very careful at this stage as you don't want to overmix, otherwise the cocoa butter will separate from the chocolate.

3   Your modelling chocolate is ready. But you need to cool it before it is ready to shape and decorate. Wrap the modelling chocolate in clingfilm and place in the fridge to cool completely. Or you can leave it wrapped on your work surface overnight.

4   Once cooled, it will be hard. Take as much or as little as you need for your decoration and knead it. With the heat from your palm, it will start to be soft and pliable. Use it as required.

MODELLING CHOCOLATE FLOWERS

Ingredient

1 batch of Modelling Chocolate

Method

1   Take the modelling chocolate out of the fridge and knead until soft. Roll it between two pieces of baking paper.

2   Use petal cutter to cut petals, then take a cupcake case or a small bowl and place a circle of baking paper at the bottom.

3   Cut a 3-4cm (1¼–1½in) disc of modelling chocolate and place on the baking paper circle. Arrange the petals on the modelling chocolate disc and press it so the petals stick with the disc. Gently press the sides of the petal to add a little texture as well as to mould.

4   Roll some modelling chocolate into a pea-sized ball and place in the middle of the flower. Decorate the sides of the ball with little rolled modelling chocolate beads as shown, opposite.

5   Continue to make more flowers from the remaining modelling chocolate. Put the flowers in the freezer for an hour or the fridge for a couple of hours to set. You can make them up to a week in advance and keep in the fridge or freezer.

Decor and accessories

Mirror glaze

CHOCOLATE MIRROR GLAZE

Ingredients

4 platinum-grade gelatine leaves
200g (7oz) granulated sugar
70ml (2½fl oz) water
2 tablespoons golden syrup
100g (3½oz) cocoa powder
100ml (3½fl oz) double (heavy) cream
100g (3½oz) dark chocolate, chopped

Tips

Always remember to freeze the cake before glazing with any mirror glaze: this will ensure the glaze sets quickly.

After glazing, let any excess glaze drip for 10–15 minutes. This will also give the glaze time to set. Then you can carefully lift the cake, using a cake lifter or two palette knives, and place it on the cake stand.

Makes enough to decorate a two-tier 20cm (8in) cake

It took me a while to master the mirror glaze. It is tricky to get the balance right: you need enough gelatine to set the glaze but not so much that it becomes rubbery. But I think I cracked the code at the end. Hopefully, you will have the most satisfying experience of pouring this glaze over your cakes!

Method

1   Soak the gelatine leaves in cold water for 5–10 minutes.
2   Meanwhile, combine the sugar, water and golden syrup in a saucepan. Place over a medium heat and bring to the boil.
3   Once all the sugar has dissolved and the liquid has been boiling for 2–3 minutes, take the pan off the heat and whisk in the cocoa powder and cream.
4   Place the chopped chocolate in heatproof measuring jug. Pour the warm sugar and cream mixture on top and mix well.
5   Squeeze the excess water out of the gelatine leaves and add them to the jug, whisking well to fully dissolve and combine.
6   Let the glaze cool down to about 33°C (91°F) before use, whisking from time to time to make sure it doesn't start to set.

COLOURED MIRROR GLAZE

Ingredients

6 platinum-grade gelatine leaves
75ml (2¾fl oz) water
150g (5½oz) caster (superfine) sugar
3 tablespoons glucose syrup
120g (4¼oz) condensed milk
150g (5½oz) white chocolate
2 teaspoons flavouring extract
   of your choice (optional)
food colouring gel (optional)

Variation

Here, I decided to show you how to make a single-colour glaze, but you can easily transform this to a marbled glazing by pouring two different-coloured glazes at the same time on the cake. Be creative and enjoy the experience!

Method

1   Soak the gelatine leaves in cold water for 5–10 minutes.
2   Meanwhile, combine the water, sugar and glucose syrup in a saucepan. Place over a mediums heat and bring to a rolling boil.
3   As the mixture starts to boil, add the condensed milk and whisk to combine, then take the pan off the heat.
4   Squeeze the excess water out of the gelatine leaves and add them to the mixture, whisking well to fully dissolve and combine.
5   Place the chopped white chocolate in a heatproof jug and pour the warm mixture over the top. Add any flavouring extract and/or food colouring you want to use, then blend with a stick blender to emulsify.
6   Set aside and leave to cool to about 30°C (86°F) before using, whisking from time to time to make sure it doesn't start to set.

3

TRANSFORMING EVERYDAY CAKES TO SHOWSTOPPING CAKES

Lemon and elderflower drizzle cake

WITH CANDIED LEMON SLICES, ELDERFLOWER CREAM AND LEMON CURD

Serves ✿ 8–10

Bake ✋ 35–40 minutes

Ingredients

For the lemon cake

200g (7oz) unsalted butter,
plus extra for greasing
200g (7oz) caster (superfine) sugar
4 medium free-range eggs
200g (7oz) self-raising (self-rising)
flour
zest of 2 lemons

For the lemon and elderflower drizzle

juice of 2 lemons
60g (2¼oz) caster sugar
2 tablespoons elderflower cordial

For the candied lemon slices

150g (5½oz) granulated sugar,
plus extra for tossing
175g (6oz) water
2 lemons, thinly sliced with
a sharp knife or mandoline

For the elderflower cream

200ml (7fl oz) whipping cream
2 tablespoons elderflower cordial

For assembly and decoration

1 batch Lemon Curd (page 62)

Tip

Keep the drizzle slightly warm before you drizzle it on the sponge. The warm syrup gets absorbed in the sponge much faster.

Method

To make the lemon and elderflower drizzle cake

1   Preheat the oven to 180°C/160°C fan/350°F/gas mark 4. Grease two 20cm (8in) cake tins with butter and line with baking paper.

2   Combine all the cake ingredients in a large mixing bowl and whisk with an electric whisk for 1 minute. Scrape down the sides of the bowl and whisk for a further minute until well combined.

3   Divide the batter between the tins and bake for 25–27 minutes, or until the cakes are shrinking away from the sides of the tins.

4   Remove from the oven and let the cakes cool in their tins for 10 minutes before transferring to a wire rack to cool completely.

5   Place the lemon juice and sugar in a saucepan over a medium heat and bring to the boil. Once it starts to boil, take the pan off the heat and stir in the elderflower syrup. Set aside.

To make the candied lemon slices

6   Place the lemon slices in saucepan of boiling water over a high heat. Boil for 5 minutes, then drain.

7   Place the measured water and sugar in a large frying pan over a medium heat. Mix to dissolve the sugar and bring to the boil.

8   Reduce the heat to low and add the lemon slices in a single layer. Simmer for 10–15 minutes, then remove from the saucepan and place on a wire rack to cool.

9   Once the slices are almost cool, toss them in some sugar, then leave to cool completely.

To make the elderflower cream

10   In a mixing bowl, whisk together the whipping cream and elderflower cordial with an electric whisk until you have soft peaks. Transfer the cream to a piping bag and set aside.

To assemble and decorate

11   Place one sponge on a 25–30cm (10–12in) cake board or stand. Set on a cake turntable then drizzle with half the syrup.

12   Cut a 1cm (½in) opening in the end of the piping bag and pipe a circular border of elderflower cream kisses around the top of the sponge. Fill the circle with 3–4 tablespoons of lemon curd.

13   Top with the second sponge then drizzle the rest of the syrup.

14   Pipe elderflower cream kisses over the top of the cake. Decorate with the lemon slices and some drops of Lemon Curd. Put the cake in the fridge to set for a couple of hours before serving. Best eaten on the same day.

Carrot, orange, ginger and pecan cake

WITH CARAMEL MASCARPONE FROSTING AND PECAN PRALINE

When I first started baking, my repertoire was limited to butter-based vanilla or lemon sponges. This carrot cake was the first oil-based cake I had ever made, for my Turkish colleague, Taner. He used to sit next to me when I first started working. Later when he got a lecture position in Turkey, I made this cake for his leaving do. I asked him what cake he would like to have, and he said carrot cake! Hence, I decided to break out of my comfort zone and made this version. I was surprised to see how moist the cake was. So, here it is: the recipe inspired by my Turkish friend is here for you all now!

Serves ✿ 16–20

Bake 🍮 40–50 minutes

Ingredients

For the carrot, orange, ginger and pecan cake

1 tablespoon butter
6–7 knobs of stem ginger
  in syrup, chopped
75g (2¾oz) dried currants
375g (13oz) self-raising (self-rising)
  flour,
  plus 1 tablespoon for dusting
5 large free-range eggs,
  at room temperature
300ml (10fl oz) sunflower oil
275g (9¾oz) dark muscovado sugar
1½ teaspoons baking powder
2 teaspoons ground cardamom
2 teaspoons ground cinnamon
½ teaspoon ground cloves
2 teaspoons ground ginger
zest of 2 oranges
300g (10½oz) carrots, grated
100g (3½oz) pecans, roasted
  and chopped

For the caramel mascarpone frosting

300g (10½oz) mascarpone,
  at room temperature
250g (9oz) cream cheese,
  at room temperature
200g (7oz) Caramel Sauce (page 44)

Method

To make the carrot, orange, ginger and pecan cake

1   Preheat the oven to 180°C/160°C fan/350°F/gas mark 4. Grease two deep 20cm (8in) loose-bottomed cake tins with butter and line with baking paper.

2   Place the chopped stem ginger and currants in a bowl. Sprinkle over the 1 tablespoon flour and toss to combine, then set aside.

3   In a large mixing bowl, whisk together the flour, eggs, sunflower oil, sugar, baking powder, ground spices and orange zest with an electric whisk until everything is well combined.

4   Add the grated carrots and pecans to the mixture, along with the stem ginger and currants, and mix gently.

5   Divide the mixture between the two lined baking tins and bake for 40–45 minutes until a skewer inserted into the centre comes out clean.

6   Remove from the oven and let the cakes cool in their tins for 10 minutes before transferring them to a wire rack to cool completely.

To make the caramel mascarpone frosting

7   In a mixing bowl, whisk together the mascarpone and cream cheese with an electric whisk until smooth and lump-free.

8   Add about 100g (3½oz) of the Caramel Sauce to the cream cheese mixture and whisk until you have a soft, spreadable consistency.

9   Spoon the frosting into a piping bag fitted with a star nozzle and set aside.

RECIPE CONTINUES NEXT PAGE ➡➡

For the pecan praline

50g (1¾oz) caster (superfine) sugar
2 teaspoons water
75g (2¾oz) pecans

To make the pecan praline

10   Heat the sugar and water in a saucepan over a medium heat. Do not stir.

11   Once the sugar starts to take on an amber colour, add the pecans. Mix well. The mixture will be very hot, so be careful. Pour the caramel-coated nuts on to a plate lined with baking paper and leave to cool.

12   Once cooled, chop into chunks.

To assemble and decorate

13   Once the cakes are cool, cut each sponge in half horizontally so that you have four sponge layers to work with. Use a little of the frosting to secure one of the sponge layers to a 25–30cm (10–12in) cake board or stand and place on a cake turntable.

14   Pipe kisses of frosting on top of the sponge and drizzle over a little of the remaining Caramel Sauce. Sprinkle over some pieces of pecan praline, then place the second sponge layer on top.

15   Repeat until all the sponges are stacked. Pipe two or three rings of frosting kisses around the outside of the sponge, then fill the rest of the space with the remaining chopped praline.

16   Transfer the cake to the fridge to set for a couple of hours before serving.

17   Due to the amount of cream cheese and cream, it is better if this cake is consumed with couple of days, and should be stored in the fridge.

Fatless sponge
WITH CREAM AND SUMMER FRUITS

This tower of feather-like sponges layered with cream and summer fruits is the showstopping cake you need for your summer party.

Serves ✿ 8–10

Bake 👆 20–23 minutes

Ingredients

For the fatless sponge

butter, for greasing
10 large free-range eggs
300g caster (superfine) sugar
Zest of 3 lemons
2 teaspoons crushed fennel seeds
300g self-raising (self-rising) flour

For the cream filling

300ml (10fl oz) double (heavy) cream
50g (1¾oz) icing (confectioner's) sugar
1 teaspoon vanilla bean paste

For assembly and decoration

600g (1lb 5oz) mixed summer berries – you can use a selection of raspberries, blueberries and blackberries; if you use strawberries, halve or quarter them
edible flowers

Method

To make the fatless sponge

1   Preheat the oven to 190°C/170°C fan/375°F/gas mark 5. Grease three 20cm (8in) cake tins with butter and line with baking paper.

2   In a mixing bowl, whisk together the eggs and sugar using an electric whisk for about 8–10 minutes until the mixture has tripled in volume. A good way to check if it's ready is to lift the whisk and draw a figure of eight with the batter. The drizzle should sit on top of the batter for at least 5–10 seconds before disappearing. This is called the ribbon stage.

3   Add the lemon zest and crushed fennel seeds, then sift the flour on top of the batter. Carefully fold them in using a spatula or metal spoon, starting at the sides of the bowl and moving quickly towards the centre. You must be gentle but quick to make sure you don't knock much air out of the batter.

4   Divide the batter equally between the prepared tins and bake for 20–23 minutes, or until the cakes start to shrink away from the sides of the tins.

5   Remove from the oven and let the cakes cool in their tins for 5–10 minutes before transferring to a wire rack to cool completely.

To make the cream filling

6   In a large mixing bowl, whip the double cream with the icing sugar and vanilla using an electric whisk, until soft peaks form. Set aside in the fridge until needed.

To assemble and decorate

7   Use a little of the cream to secure one of the sponges on a 25–30cm (10–12in) cake board or cake stand on a cake turntable. Spread about a third of the cream over the sponge, then scatter some summer berries over the top.

8   Place the second sponge on top and repeat with more whipped cream and berries

9   Finally, top with the third sponge and spread the remaining on top. Scatter the remaining berries and decorate with edible flowers.

10   Although this cake is delicious and light when fresh, the fat-free sponges tend to dry out quickly, and it uses a lot of double cream, so it is best not to keep it for more than a day.

Mango and ginger cake

WITH SPICED MANGO MASCARPONE FROSTING, MANGO COULIS AND FRESH MANGO

This mangoey mango cake reminds me of summers in India. The aroma, the colour, the flavour, it just brings back so many joyful memories.

Serves ✿ 8–10

Bake 🧤 20–25 minutes

Ingredients

For the mango and ginger cake

1 large, firm mango (about 200g/7oz), flesh, roughly chopped into 5mm–1 cm (¼–½in) pieces

6–7 knobs of stem ginger, roughly chopped

300g (10½oz) self-raising flour, plus 1 tablespoon for dusting

6 medium free-range eggs

300g (10½oz) caster (superfine) sugar

300g (10½oz) unsalted butter, plus extra for greasing

½ teaspoon salt

zest of 2 limes

2 teaspoons ground cardamom

75g (2½oz) mango purée

For the spiced mango mascarpone frosting

350g (12oz) mascarpone

100ml (3½fl oz) double (heavy) cream

200g (7oz) mango purée, plus a little extra if needed

50g (1¾oz) icing (confectioner's) sugar

½ teaspoon ground nutmeg

2 teaspoons ground cardamom

For the mango coulis (optional)

75gl (2½oz) mango purée

25ml (¾fl oz) water

For assembly and decoration

2 ripe mangoes, chopped into 1cm (½in) pieces

handful of pomegranate seeds

Tip

If you don't have any mango purée, blitz the flesh from 2 mangoes to get enough purée for the frosting and coulis.

Method

To make the mango and ginger cake

1   Preheat the oven to 180°C/160°C fan/350°F/gas mark 4. Grease three 20cm (8in) cake tins with butter and line with baking paper. As the cake is going to be a 'naked' cake, it's important to line the sides of the tins as well to get a nice clean finish.

2   Place the chopped mango and stem ginger in a bowl. Scatter over the 1 tablespoon of flour and toss to coat, then set aside.

3   In a mixing bowl, whisk the remaining sponge ingredients with an electric whisk for 1 minute until well combined.

4   Add the flour-coated chopped mango and stem ginger and gently fold into the batter.

5   Divide the batter between the prepared tins and bake for 25–30 minutes until a skewer inserted into the middle comes out clean.

6   Remove from the oven. Let the sponges cool in their tins for 10 minutes before turning out on to a wire rack to cool completely.

To make the spiced mango mascarpone frosting

7   In a mixing bowl, whisk together all the frosting ingredients using an electric whisk. The mixture will thicken as you whisk, creating a smooth, spreadable frosting. If the frosting is too thick, add a few extra tablespoons of mango purée. If it is too runny add couple of tablespoons of more mascarpone.

To assemble and decorate

8   Use a little frosting to secure one of the sponges on a 25–30cm (10–12in) cake board or cake stand and place on a cake turntable.

9   Spread about a third of the frosting on top of the sponge, then scatter over a third of the chopped mango and pomegranate seeds.

10 Top with the second sponge, followed by another third of the frosting and more chopped mango and pomegranate seeds.

11 Place the third sponge on top and spread it with the rest of the frosting. Decorate with the remaining chopped mango and pomegranate seeds.

12 Make the coulis by mixing together the mango purée and water in a small jug or bowl. Pour this over the cake just before serving.

Apple and walnut cake
WITH CINNAMON CREAM CHEESE FILLING

This apple cake with a bit of ginger and walnut with caramel sauce is just what you need on chilly autumn evenings. But it is a great way to use up windfall apples in the late summer too. Hope you enjoy this treat.

Serves ✿ 10–12

Bake 🥄 40–50 minutes

Ingredients

For the apple and walnut cake

2 Bramley or other cooking apples (about 400–500g/14oz–1lb 2 oz before peeling and coring), peeled, cored and roughly chopped into 1.5–2cm (⅝–¾in) cubes

125g (4½oz) walnuts, roughly chopped

280g (10oz) self-raising (self-rising) flour, plus 2 tablespoons for dusting

zest of 1 lemon

6 medium free-range eggs

150g (5½oz) caster (superfine) sugar

150g (5½oz) dark brown sugar

300g (10½oz) unsalted butter, plus extra for greasing

50g (1¾oz) Greek yogurt

1½ teaspoons baking powder

2 teaspoons ground cinnamon

2 teaspoons ground ginger

For the cinnamon cream cheese filling

1 batch Cream Cheese Frosting (page 38)

1½ teaspoons ground cinnamon

For assembly and decoration

½ batch Apple and Cinnamon Compote (page 56)

½ batch Caramel Sauce (page 44)

1 Granny Smith apple, sliced into thin wedges and sprinkled with lemon juice to avoid browning

Method

To make the apple and walnut cake

1   Preheat the oven to 180°C/160°C fan/350°F/gas mark 4. Grease three 20cm (8in) cake tins with butter and line with baking paper.

2   Place the chopped apples and walnuts in a small bowl. Sprinkle over the 2 tablespoons of flour and toss to coat, then set aside.

3   Combine the remaining ingredients in a large mixing bowl and whisk using an electric whisk for 1–1½ minutes until everything is well combined. Scrape down the sides of the bowl and whisk for a further minute.

4   Gently fold in the flour-coated apple and walnuts, then divide the batter equally between the prepared tins.

5   Bake for 35–40 minutes, or until a skewer inserted into the middle comes out clean.

6   Remove from the oven and let the cakes cool in their tins for 10 minutes. Then turn them out on to a wire rack to cool completely.

To make the cinnamon cream cheese filling

7   In a mixing bowl, whisk together the Cream Cheese Frosting and cinnamon with an electric whisk for 10–15 seconds until well combined. Transfer the frosting to a piping bag fitted with a St Honoré nozzle.

To assemble and decorate

8   Use a little frosting to secure one of the sponges on a 25–30cm (10–12in) cake board or cake stand and place on a cake turntable.

9   Cut a 1cm (½in) opening in the end of the piping bag and pipe kisses of cinnamon cream cheese frosting around the top of the sponge. Fill the middle of the frosting ring with half the Apple and Cinnamon Compote and drizzle some Caramel Sauce over the top.

10 Place the second sponge on top and repeat the step above with another ring of frosting and the rest of the Compote. Drizzle with some Caramel Sauce and top with the third sponge.

11 Pipe the rest of the frosting on to the top of the cake in a circular fashion, starting from the outside and working inwards.

12 Finally, arrange some thin wedges of apple on top of the cake, and drizzle with a little more Caramel Sauce to finish.

Lemon and blueberry cake

WITH LEMON CURD AND BLUEBERRY COMPOTE

I first made this cake for my colleague David's surprise birthday, for his love of lemon cake as well as blueberries. Since then, all my colleagues now love this cake, so I hope you will love it too.

Serves ✿ 8–10

Bake ✿ 35–40 minutes

Ingredients

For the lemon and blueberry cake

150g (5½oz) fresh or frozen
    blueberries
300g (10½oz) self-raising flour,
    plus 1 tablespoon for dusting
300g (10½oz) unsalted butter,
    at room temperature, plus extra
    for greasing
300g (10½oz) caster (superfine)
    sugar
6 large free-range eggs,
    at room temperature
90g (3¼oz) Greek yogurt
½ teaspoon baking powder
1 tablespoon crushed fennel seeds
zest of 3 lemons
1 teaspoon lemon extract

For the syrup

80g (2¾oz) caster sugar
juice of 2 lemons

For assembly and decoration

1 batch Lemon Curd (page 62)
1½ batches American Buttercream
    (page 32), flavoured with
    2 teaspoons lemon extract
2 batches Blueberry and Lemon
    Compote (page 58)
100–150g (3½–5½oz) fresh
    blueberries

Tip

I prefer to use frozen blueberries to bake with the cake batter. During the cooking they defrost as well as get a little soft, but not so much that they bleed inside the cake.

Method

To make the lemon and blueberry cake

1 Preheat the oven to 180°C/160°C fan/350°F/gas mark 4. Grease three 20cm (8in) cake tins with butter and line with baking paper.

2 Place the blueberries in a small bowl and scatter over the 1 tablespoon of flour. Toss to coat and set aside.

3 In a mixing bowl, whisk together the remaining cake ingredients with an electric whisk for 30 seconds to 1 minute until combined.

4 Fold in the flour-coated blueberries.

5 Divide the batter between the prepared tins and bake for 25–30 minutes until a skewer inserted into the middle comes out clean.

6 Remove from the oven and let the cakes cool in their tins for 5 minutes before turning out on to a wire rack to cool completely.

To make the syrup

7 Heat the lemon juice and sugar in a small saucepan over a medium heat until it reaches 105°C (221°F) and is bubbling. Take off the heat and use while still warm.

To assemble and decorate

8 Use a little of the American Buttercream to secure one of the sponges on a 25–30cm (10–12in) cake board or cake stand and place on a cake turntable. Drizzle with a third of the lemon syrup.

9 Spoon two-thirds of the Buttercream into a piping bag and leave the rest in the bowl. Cut a 1cm (½in) opening in the end of the bag and pipe a border of buttercream around the top of the sponge. Fill with the Lemon Curd and top with a thin layer of buttercream.

10 Place the second cake on top and drizzle with another third of the syrup. Pipe another ring of buttercream around the edge, then fill the inside with half the Blueberry and Lemon Compote. Top with another thin layer of buttercream, then the third sponge.

11 Drizzle the third sponge with the rest of the syrup, then coat the top and sides of the cake with the remaining Buttercream from the bowl. You want the sides to look smooth, but still have some of the cake texture peeking through the buttercream.

12 Pipe a circular border of buttercream kisses around the top of the cake, if you want you can use a star piping nozzle like in the photo or keep it simple without any piping nozzle. Pour the remaining Blueberry and Lemon Compote into the middle and top with fresh blueberries.

13 This can be stored in the fridge for a couple of days.

Spiced carrot and walnut cake

WITH WHISKED MISO CARAMEL, CREAM CHEESE FROSTING, MISO CARAMEL DRIP AND HONEYCOMB

If you like carrot cakes, you will love this cake. It is an all-in-one cake, so you pour all the ingredients in a mixing bowl and whisk until all is combined well. It is a relatively simple technique that results in the beautifully soft carroty sponges. The twist in this cake comes in with the miso caramel. I will be honest; I am relatively new to using miso in baking. It is inspired by Crystelle Pereira's generous use of miso from the 2021 *Great British Bake Off*. And it does work. The salty umami-ness of miso works beautifully with the sweet caramel sauce, cream cheese frosting and carrot sponges. This cake is crowned with honeycomb shards. For me, this the perfect autumn showstopping cake, for any occasion from birthdays to Halloween to Thanksgiving.

Serves ✿ 10–12

Bake 🌢 1 hour–1 hour 15 minutes

Ingredients

For the spiced carrot and walnut cake

300g (10½oz) unsalted butter, plus extra for greasing
6 medium free-range eggs
275g (9¾oz) dark muscovado sugar
400g (14oz) self-raising flour
2 teaspoons ground cardamom
1 teaspoon ground cinnamon
½ teaspoons ground nutmeg
¾ teaspoon baking powder
400g (14oz) carrots, grated
150g (5½oz) walnuts, roughly chopped

For the whisked miso caramel and miso caramel drip

1 batch Miso Caramel (variation, page 44)

For the cream cheese frosting

1–2 batches Cream Cheese Frosting (page 58)

For the decoration

1 batch of Honeycomb (page 71)

Method

To make the spiced carrot and walnut cake

1   Preheat the oven to 180°C/160°C fan/350°F/gas mark 4. Grease three 20cm (8in) cake tins with butter and line with baking paper.

2   Place all the cake ingredients (except carrots and walnuts) in a large mixing bowl and whisk using an electric whisk for a couple of minutes. Scrape down the sides of the bowl and whisk for another minute. Now, add the grated carrot and chopped walnuts and gently fold them into the batter, trying not to knock out too much air.

3   Divide the batter equally between the prepared tins and bake for 40–45 minutes, or until a skewer inserted into the middle comes out clean.

4   Remove from the oven and let the cakes cool in their tins for 5–10 minutes before turning out on to a wire rack to cool completely.

To make the whisked miso caramel

5   Remove a couple of tablespoons of the Miso Caramel and set aside to use for the drip. Pour the rest into a heatproof bowl and cover with clingfilm, making sure the clingfilm is touching the surface of the caramel. Place in the fridge for 45–60 minutes.

6   Once the caramel is chilled and firm to the touch, take it out of the fridge and whisk using an electric whisk until it is fluffy and light.

RECIPE CONTINUES NEXT PAGE ➡➡

You can make the cake a day earlier with the drip and store it in the fridge. Decorate with the honeycombs on top at the last minute.

To assemble and decorate

7 Spoon the Cream Cheese Frosting in a piping bag and cut a 1cm (½in) opening in the other.

8 Use a little frosting to secure one of the sponges on a 25–30cm (10–12in) cake board. Place the cake boardon on a cake turntable.

9 Pipe a circular border of frosting around the edge of the first sponge, rotating the cake on the turntable to help you. Fill the frosting circle with a few tablespoons of the whisked Miso Caramel, then pipe a thin layer of frosting on top and smooth using a palette knife. Top with the second sponge.

10 Repeat the step above with more frosting and the rest of the whisked Miso Caramel, then place the third sponge on top.

11 Use the rest of the frosting to coat the sides and top of the cake, then place in the fridge for an hour to allow the frosting to set.

12 Pour the rest of the Miso Caramel on top of the cake and spread using a pallet knife. Encourage some of the caramel to drip from the sides of the cake.

13 Keep the cake chilled, but remove from the fridge about an hour before serving and decorate the top with broken shards of honeycomb.

14 This cake can be kept in the fridge for couple days.

Chocolate and hazelnut cake

WITH CHOCOLATE AND HAZELNUT FROSTING

If you like chocolate and hazelnut, you have got to make this cake. It is simple and easy to make and extremely delicious. I haven't used any hazelnut liqueur in this cake, but if you have some lying around, a tablespoon of it, drizzled over each sponge, will take this cake to a different level. The filling and frosting of this cake is fairly straightforward with the use of your favourite brand of chocolate hazelnut spread in a buttercream. Decorate the cake with more hazelnuts. I like to slice the nuts in 3–4 sections horizontally and arrange them around the top and bottom edge of the cake. But you can decorate however you want – be creative and enjoy the process of decorating the cake.

Serves ✿ 8–10

Bake ❧ 30–35 minutes

Ingredients

For the chocolate and hazelnut cake

150g (5½oz) blanched hazelnuts
200g (7oz) unsalted butter,
    plus extra for greasing
200g (7oz) dark brown sugar
4 medium free-range eggs
125g (4½oz) self-raising (self-rising)
    flour
1 teaspoon baking powder
50g (1¾oz) cocoa powder
90g (3¼oz) Greek yogurt

**For the chocolate and
hazelnut frosting**

250g (9oz) salted butter
200g (7oz) icing (confectioner's)
    sugar
200g (7oz) chocolate and
    hazelnut spread

For the decoration

100g (3½oz) toasted
    hazelnuts, sliced

Method

To make the chocolate and hazelnut cake

1   Preheat the oven to 180°C/160°C fan/350°F/gas mark 4. Grease two 20cm (8in) cake tins with butter and line with baking paper.

2   Place the hazelnuts in a baking tray and roast for 5–10 minutes until golden and fragrant. Remove from the oven (but leave the oven on) and leave the hazelnuts to cool completely.

3   Once cool, weigh out 50g (1¾oz) of the roasted hazelnuts and set aside to use in the filling. Weigh out another 75g (2¾oz) of the hazelnuts and blitz in a food processor to a fine powder. Roughly chop the remaining hazelnuts.

4   In a mixing bowl, whisk together the butter and sugar with an electric whisk for 5 minutes until light and fluffy. Scrape down the sides of the bowl and whisk again for another 3 minutes.

5   Add the eggs, one at a time, whisking well between each addition.

6   Once all the eggs are incorporated, sift in the flour, baking powder and cocoa powder, and sprinkle in the ground hazelnuts. Fold to combine well without knocking too much air out of the batter.

7   Finally, add the roughly chopped hazelnuts and yogurt and mix well.

8   Divide the batter between the prepared tins and bake for 25–30 minutes, or until a skewer inserted into the middle comes out clean.

9   Remove the cakes from the oven and leave to cool in their tins for 10 minutes before turning out on to a wire rack to cool completely.

RECIPE CONTINUES NEXT PAGE ▶▶

To make the chocolate and hazelnut frosting

10   In a mixing bowl, beat the butter using an electric whisk for about 5 minutes. Sift in half the icing sugar and beat well for another 2–3 minutes.

11   Scrape down the sides of the bowl and add the rest of the icing sugar. Beat thoroughly for another couple of minutes.

12   Add the chocolate and hazelnut spread and whisk to combine, remembering to scrape down the sides of the bowl.

To assemble and decorate

13   Use a little of the frosting to secure one of the sponges on a 25–30cm (10–12in) cake board or cake stand and place on a cake turntable. Spoon 2–3 generous tablespoons of frosting on top of the sponge and spread it evenly.

14   Chop the reserved hazelnuts and scatter a tablespoon of them over the frosting before topping with the second sponge.

15   Use half of the remaining frosting to coat the sides and top of the cake with a crumb coating, spreading it out using a palette knife.

16   Put the cake in fridge to chill for 30 minutes, then remove it from the fridge and use the remaining frosting to give it a final coat.

17   If you have a cake turntable, here is a quick and easy trick to decorate this cake: with the turntable rotating, touch the outer edge of the top of the cake with the tip of the palette knife and move it inwards as the cake rotates. This will create a beautiful spiral pattern on top.

18   Return the cake to the fridge to cool and set completely. Decorate the top and bottom edge of the cake with sliced hazelnuts before serving.

19   This cake will be fine, covered, at room temperature for a day, or for a couple days in the fridge. Remember to bring to room temperature before serving.

Coconut and lime cake

WITH COCONUT SWISS MERINGUE BUTTERCREAM AND LIME CURD

Serves ✿ 8–10

Bake ✋ 45–50 minutes

Ingredients

For the coconut and lime cake

100g (3½oz) desiccated (shredded)
  coconut
250g (9oz) unsalted butter, plus
  extra for greasing
325g (11½oz) caster (superfine) sugar
zest of 3 limes
80g (2¾oz) coconut oil
6 medium free-range eggs
275g (9¾oz) self-raising (self-rising)
  flour
3 tablespoons coconut cream

**For the coconut Swiss meringue
buttercream**

4 large free-range egg whites
300g (10½oz) caster sugar
200g (7oz) salted butter
200g (7oz) unsalted butter
2–3 teaspoons coconut extract
2 teaspoons ground cardamom

For assembly and decoration

1 batch Lime Curd (variation,
  page 62)
2–3 tablespoons toasted
  coconut flakes

Method

To make the coconut and lime cake

1   Preheat the oven to 180°C/160°C fan/350°F/gas mark 4. Grease three 20cm (8in) cake tins with butter and line with baking paper.

2   In a dry frying pan, toast the desiccated coconut over a low heat for 2–3 minutes until fragrant. Leave to cool.

3   In a large mixing bowl, combine all the cake ingredients, including the toasted desiccated coconut, and whisk using an electric whisk for a couple of minutes. Scrape down the sides of the bowl and whisk again for a further minute until you have a light and fluffy batter.

4   Divide the batter equally between the prepared baking tins and bake for 25–30 minutes, or until a skewer inserted into the middle comes out clean. Let the cakes cool in their tins for 10 minutes before turning out on to a wire rack to cool completely.

5   Make the coconut Swiss meringue buttercream according to the instructions on page 34, but using the quantities given here. Add the coconut extract and ground cardamom at the end, instead of the vanilla, and mix well to combine.

6   Once the buttercream is ready, spoon half into a piping bag and leave the rest in the bowl, covered.

To assemble and decorate

7   Use buttercream to secure one of the sponges on a 25–30cm (10–12in) cake board or stand and place on a cake turntable.

8   Cut a 1cm (½in) opening in the end of the piping bag and pipe a circular border of buttercream around the top of the sponge. Fill the middle of the buttercream ring with 2–3 tablespoons of Lime Curd, then spread a thin layer of buttercream on top of the curd.

9   Place the second sponge on top and repeat the step above, finishing with the third sponge.

10 Coat the top and sides of the cake to lock any loose crumbs with half the remaining buttercream from the piping bag, spreading it with a palette knife. Chill the crumb-coated cake in the fridge for 45 minutes, or pop it in the freezer for 15 minutes.

11 Remove from the fridge or freezer and give it a final coating with the remaining buttercream, using a palette knife or a cake scraper to make the sides and top smooth. Return to the fridge for a further 45 minutes, or to the freezer for 15 minutes.

12 Once the buttercream has set, decorate the top of the cake with the toasted coconut flakes.

13 Store this cake covered in the fridge for a couple of days, but be sure to take it out of the fridge a couple of hours before serving.

Chocolate, orange and caramel cake

WITH CARAMEL FILLING, CHOCOLATE AND CARAMEL GANACHE AND ORANGE SYRUP

The combination of chocolate and salted caramel is a marriage made in heaven. This chocolate sandwich cake has a salted caramel filling, and it's also coated with chocolate and caramel ganache – a true crowd-pleaser. I made this for a Macmillan Coffee Morning, and everyone loved it.

Serves ✿ 8–10

Bake ♥ 30–33 minutes

Ingredients

For the chocolate, orange and caramel cake

90g (3¼oz) cocoa powder
140ml (4¾fl oz) warm milk
zest of 2 large oranges and juice
 of 1 orange
500g (1lb 2oz) dark brown sugar
90g (3¼oz) Greek yogurt
170g (6oz) unsalted butter,
 at room temperature,
 plus extra for greasing
5 medium free-range eggs
300g (10½oz) self-raising (self-rising)
 flour
½ teaspoon baking powder

For the caramel filling

1 batch Salted Caramel Sauce
 (page 44)

For the chocolate and caramel ganache

300g (10½oz) dark
 chocolate, chopped
250ml (9fl oz) Salted Caramel
 Sauce (above)

For the orange syrup

juice of 2 oranges
60g (2¼oz) caster sugar

Method

To make the chocolate, orange and caramel cake

1 Preheat the oven to 180°C/160°C fan/350°F/gas mark 4. Grease three 20cm (8in) cake tins with butter and line with baking paper.

2 Place the cocoa and warm milk in a mixing bowl and mix well using an electric whisk to form a thick paste.

3 Add the remaining ingredients (in the order listed) and whisk for a couple of minutes to mix thoroughly. Scrape down the sides of the bowl and whisk for another minute to fully combine.

4 Divide the batter evenly between the prepared tins and bake for 30–33 minutes or until a skewer inserted into the middle comes out clean.

5 Let the cakes cool in their tins for 10 minutes before turning out on to a wire rack to cool completely.

To make the chocolate and caramel ganache

6 Place the chopped dark chocolate in a bowl and pour 250ml (9fl oz) hot (80–85°C/176–185°F) Salted Caramel Sauce on top. Let it sit for 5 minutes, then stir well to mix.

7 Place it in the fridge for a couple of hours to chill. When the ganache is cooled, take it out of the fridge and whisk using an electric whisk, until it reaches a spreadable consistency.

8 Spoon about one-third of the whipped ganache into a piping bag and leave the rest in the bowl.

To make the orange syrup

9 Heat the orange juice and sugar in a small saucepan over a medium heat until all the sugar has dissolved and the mixture is starting to boil. Take off the heat and set aside.

RECIPE CONTINUES NEXT PAGE ▶▶

To assemble and decorate

10 Use a little ganache to secure one of the sponges on to a 25–30cm (10–12in) cake board or cake stand and place on a cake turntable.

11 Cut a 1cm (1/2in) opening in the end of the piping bag and pipe a circular border of ganache around the top of the sponge

12 Spoon one-third of the Salted Caramel Sauce into the middle of the ganache ring and spread out evenly.

13 Top with the second sponge. Drizzle with a few tablespoons of syrup, then repeat step 12, topping it with the third sponge.

14 Transfer half of the remaining ganache in the bowl into a piping bag fitted with a star nozzle.

15 Coat the top and sides of the cake with a crumb coating using some of the ganache still in the bowl. Place the cake in the freezer for 15 minutes to set.

16 Once set, remove from the freezer and give it a final, smooth coating using the rest of the ganache in the bowl.

17 Now use the ganache in the piping bag with the star nozzle to pipe 2–3 circles of kisses around the top of the cake. You can do some rosettes too, if you like. Fill the middle of the circle with the rest of the caramel sauce.

18 Chill the cake for an hour to set, but remember to take it out of the fridge at least an hour before serving.

19 You can keep this cake in the fridge for a couple of days.

Lemon and raspberry cake

WITH RASPBERRY JAM AND WHITE CHOCOLATE ITALIAN MERINGUE BUTTERCREAM

Lemon and raspberry is my favourite flavour combination – many of my recipes contain these two ingedients but among them all, this cake is probably my number one. The sweet tartness of the raspberries with lemon's citrus fragrance works beautifully. It is simple yet showstopping on its own in flavour as well as in decoration. The decoration on the sides is called watercolour icing and it works great with any pastel shades. Here, some of the buttercream is mixed with ground freeze-dried raspberries. However, feel free to use a drop of gel pink/red food colouring to get similar shades.

Serves ✿ 8–10

Bake ▼ 45–60 minutes

Ingredients

For the lemon and raspberry cake

150g (5½oz) frozen raspberries
300g (10½oz) self-raising flour,
　plus 1 tablespoon for dusting
300g (10½oz) unsalted butter,
　at room temperature,
　plus extra for greasing
6 medium free-range eggs
zest of 4 lemons
300g (10½oz) caster (superfine)
　sugar
1 teaspoon baking powder

For the raspberry jam

1 batch Raspberry Jam (page 60)

For the white chocolate Italian meringue buttercream

4 medium free-range egg whites
200g (7oz) caster sugar
80ml (2¾fl oz) water
170g (6oz) salted butter
300g (10½oz) unsalted butter
1 teaspoon vanilla bean paste
200g (7oz) white chocolate, melted
　and cooled
1 tablespoon freeze-dried raspberries,
　ground into a powder

For decoration

White Chocolate Shards (page 77)

Method

To make the lemon and raspberry cake

1　Preheat the oven to 180°C/160°C fan/350°F/gas mark 4. Grease three 15cm (6in) cake tins with butter and line with baking paper.

2　Place the frozen raspberries in a bowl. Sprinkle over the 1 tablespoon of flour, then toss to coat and set aside. Coating the berries in flour helps stop them from sinking to the bottom of the batter.

3　In a large mixing bowl, combine all the remaining ingredients for the cake and whisk together for 1 minute. Scrape down the sides of the bowl and whisk for another minute.

4　Carefully fold the flour-coated raspberries into the batter.

5　Divide the batter equally between the prepared tins. Bake for 40–45 minutes, or until a skewer inserted into the middle comes out clean.

6　Remove the cakes from the oven and leave to cool in their tins for 10 minutes before turning out on to a wire rack to cool completely.

To make the white chocolate Italian meringue buttercream

7　Make an Italian meringue buttercream according to the recipe on page 33, but using the quantities given here.

8　Remove about 3 heaped tablespoons of the buttercream from the mixing bowl and place in a separate bowl with the freeze-dried raspberry powder. Mix together and transfer into a piping bag, then set aside.

9　Whisk the rest of the buttercream with the cooled melted white chocolate. Spoon half of this white chocolate buttercream into a piping bag and leave the rest in the bowl.

RECIPE CONTINUES NEXT PAGE ▶▶

To assemble and decorate

10   Use a little buttercream to secure one of the sponges on a 20cm (8in) cake board. Place the cake board on a cake turntable.

11   Cut a 1cm (½in) opening in the end of the piping bag and pipe a circular border of white chocolate buttercream around the top of the sponge, rotating the cake on the turntable to help you. Fill the inside of the buttercream ring with a couple of tablespoons of Raspberry Jam.

12   Place the second sponge on the top, then repeat the step above with more white chocolate buttercream and jam. Finish by stacking the third sponge on top.

13   Coat the sides and top of the cake with a crumb coating of the white chocolate buttercream from the bowl. Place the cake in the fridge for about 45 minutes to set, or in the freezer for 15 minutes.

14   Once set, take it out of the fridge or freezer and coat the sides and top with the rest of the buttercream. Smooth it with a cake scraper or a palette knife.

15   Pipe some blobs of raspberry buttercream around the sides of the cake, then use a cake scraper to smooth and smear it into the white chocolate buttercream with just a few swift swipes. This will create a watercolour effect on the sides of the cake. If you try to smooth it too much, you will lose the effect.

16   Pipe kisses on top of the cake with the remaining white chocolate buttercream, then decorate with a few White Chocolate Shards. The cake can be stored in the fridge for a couple of days.

Coconut and cardamom genoise

WITH MANGO PASTRY CRÈME AND WHITE CHOCOLATE MASCARPONE FROSTING

This is my mum's favourite cake and made with all her favourite flavours: coconut, cardamom and mango. Growing up in India we always had different coconut desserts which are flavoured with cardamom. The sponges remind me of those flavours. The cake is filled with a mango pastry crème and coated with a white chocolate mascarpone frosting. Being a huge fan of mangoes, I have been overly generous with them in the decoration, but you can use as few or as many mangoes you want.

Serves ✿ 8–10

Bake ❧ 45–55 minutes

Ingredients

For the coconut and cardamom genoise

10 medium free-range eggs
300g (10½oz) caster sugar
200g (7oz) plain flour
3 teaspoons ground cardamom
150g (5½oz) desiccated (shredded) coconut, lightly toasted
50g (1¾oz) unsalted butter, melted and cooled, plus extra for greasing
50g (1¾oz) coconut oil, melted and cooled
zest of 1 lime

For the mango pastry crème

100ml (3½fl oz) double (heavy) cream
150g (5½oz) mango purée
2 teaspoons ground cardamom
3 medium free-range egg yolks
40g (1½oz) (1½oz) dark brown sugar
25g (1oz) cornflour (cornstarch)
70g (2½oz) salted butter, chilled and cubed
zest of 1 lime

For assembly and decoration

1–1½ batch White Chocolate Mascarpone Frosting (variation, page 37)
3 mangoes, peeled, stoned and diced
2–3 tablespoons lightly toasted coconut flakes

Method

To make the coconut and cardamom genoise

1   Preheat the oven to 190°C/170°C fan/375°F/gas mark 5. Grease three 20cm (8in) loose-bottomed cake tins with butter and line with baking paper.

2   In a large mixing bowl, whisk the eggs and sugar using an electric whisk for at least 7–8 minutes until the mixture reaches the ribbon stage (see page 15).

3   Sift the flour and ground cardamom over the top, then add the toasted desiccated coconut. Fold in gently with a metal spoon, being careful not to knock out too much air.

4   In a small mixing bowl, combine the butter with the coconut oil and lime zest. Add a couple of tablespoons of the batter and mix well, then slowly drizzle the butter mix into the batter and fold in to combine.

5   Divide the batter equally between the prepared baking tins. Bake for 23–25 minutes until the cake starts to shrink away from the sides of the tin.

6   Remove from the oven and let the cakes cool in their tins for 10 minutes before turning out on to a wire rack to cool completely.

To make the mango pastry crème

7   Place the cream, mango purée and cardamom in a saucepan over a medium heat until just about to boil, but take it off the heat before it boils.

8   In a mixing bowl, whisk together the egg yolks, sugar and cornflour with a balloon whisk until pale and thick.

9   Add the warm cream and mango mixture and whisk well to combine, then transfer the mixture back to the saucepan and place over a medium heat. After 5–7 minutes, it will start to thicken. Once this happens, whisk vigorously to create a smooth, lump-free pastry crème.

RECIPE CONTINUES NEXT PAGE ➡➡

10 Take the pan off the heat and whisk in the butter, along with the lime zest.

11 Pour into a heatproof bowl and cover with clingfilm, making sure the clingfilm touches the surface of the pastry crème. Leave to cool completely.

To assemble and decorate

12 If the mango pastry crème has set, remove the clingfilm and give it a good whisk to loosen.

13 Place half of the White Chocolate Mascarpone Frosting in a piping bag and set aside, leaving the remaining frosting in the mixing bowl.

14 Use a little of the White Chocolate Mascarpone Frosting to secure the first sponge on a 25–30cm (10–12in cake board or cake stand and place on a cake turntable.

15 Cut the tip of the second piping bag to create a 1cm (½in) opening and pipe a circular border of White Chocolate Mascarpone Frosting around the top of the sponge. Fill the inside of the frosting ring with half of the mango pastry crème.

16 Place the second sponge on top, then repeat the previous step, piping a ring of frosting and filling it with the remaining pastry crème.

17 Top with the third sponge, then coat the side and top of the cake with half of the frosting from the bowl, using a palette knife to spread it out. Place the cake in the fridge for about an hour or in the freezer for 20 minutes to set.

18 Remove the cake from the fridge or freezer and coat the cake with the rest of the frosting from the bowl. Now use the top of the palette knife to make some vertical strokes in the frosting all around the sides of the cake, adding a bit of texture. Return the cake to the fridge or freezer for an hour to set completely.

19 Once set, decorate the top of the cake with the diced mango.

20 Scatter some toasted coconut flakes on the top to finish.

21 This cake can be kept in the fridge for up to a maximum of two days but it tastes better fresh with the fresh mangoes. If you are planning to keep the cake in the fridge, sprinkle some lemon juice on top of the chopped mangoes to stop them getting oxidised.

Strawberries and cream cake

WITH WHITE CHOCOLATE BAVAROIS, FRESH STRAWBERRIES AND MERINGUE KISSES

The first time I made this cake was for a Wimbledon tennis viewing party which must be celebrated with strawberries and cream. Hence, this cake, where the strawberry sponges are sandwiched with white chocolate bavarois and decorated with meringue kisses. Can it be any more summery? I hope this cake will be the attraction in many of your summer Wimbledon viewing parties.

Serves ✿ 10–12

Bake 🍴 2 hours–2 hours 30 minutes

Ingredients

For the strawberry cake

250g (9oz) frozen strawberries
100g (3½oz) strawberry jam
200g (7oz) unsalted butter,
   plus extra for greasing
4 medium free-range eggs
150g (5½oz) caster (superfine) sugar
200g (7oz) self-raising (self-rising)
   flour
1 teaspoon baking powder
1 teaspoon strawberry flavouring

For the meringue kisses

1 large free-range egg white
1 teaspoon lemon juice
50g (1¾oz) caster sugar
red food colouring gel

For the white chocolate bavarois

½ batch White Chocolate Bavarois
   (page 43)

For assembly and decoration

1 batch Swiss Meringue Buttercream
   (page 34)
100g (3½oz) fresh strawberries,
   strawberries, hulled and sliced

Method

To make the strawberry cake

1   Place the frozen strawberries in a saucepan over a medium heat. Cover and cook for 10 minutes, then take off the lid and mash the strawberries with a potato masher. Continue to cook until reduced by half.

2   Add the strawberry jam and reduce by half once again. You will need about 100g (3½oz) in total of this strawberry reduction. Leave to cool to room temperature.

3   In a large mixing bowl, whisk together all the cake ingredients, including the cooled strawberry reduction, using an electric whisk for about 1 minute. Scrape down the sides of the bowl and whisk for another minute.

4   Preheat the oven to 180°C/160°C fan/350°F/gas mark 4. Grease two 20cm (8in) cake tins with butter and line with baking paper.

5   Divide the batter equally between the prepared ed tins and bake for 30–35 minutes, or until a skewer inserted into the middle comes out clean.

6   Remove from the oven and let the cakes cool in their tins for 10 minutes before turning out on to a wire rack to cool completely.

To make the meringue kisses

7   Reduce the oven temperature to 120°C/100°C fan/250°F/gas mark ½ and line a baking sheet with baking paper.

8   In a clean bowl, whisk together the egg white and lemon juice with an electric whisk until soft peaks form. Start adding the caster sugar, 1 tablespoon at a time. Whisk thoroughly in between each addition to ensure all the sugar is incorporated fully. You will end up with a stiff, glossy meringue.

9   Fit a piping bag with a star nozzle and paint the inside of the bag with a few strokes of red food colouring. Fill the piping bag with the meringue.

10 Pipe meringue kisses on to the prepared baking sheet. Bake for 45 minutes–1 hour, then turn off the oven and leave the meringues to cool inside, with the door ajar.

RECIPE CONTINUES NEXT PAGE ➡➡

To assemble and decorate

11 Line the sides of a 20cm (8in) loose-bottomed cake tin with a strip of acetate 10–12cm (4–6in) high.

12 Place the first strawberry cake inside and press firmly.

13 Pour the White Chocolate Bavarois on top and smooth using a pallet knife. Place the second sponge on top.

14 Place it in the fridge to set over night or minimum 4–6 hours.

15 Once set, remove it from the fridge and carefully lift the cake out of the tin.

16 Gently unwrap the acetate from the sides of the cake.

17 Coat the sides of the cake with half the Swiss Meringue Buttercream and smooth using a pallet knife or a cake scraper. Return the cake to the fridge to set for 30 minutes.

18 Remove from the fridge to coat with the remaining buttercream, again using a pallet knife or cake scraper to achieve smooth edges, before returning it to the fridge for a further 30 minutes.

19 Once removed from the fridge, decorate the sides of the cake with slices of strawberries as shown in the photo. A small amount of buttercream may be used to make them stick if necessary.

20 Finally arrange the meringue kisses in a circle on top of the cake.

21 Keep the cake chilled until you need to serve it. It can be stored in the fridge for a couple of days, but after this the meringues will start become soft.

Lemon genoise

WITH FRENCH MERINGUE, RASPBERRY CURD AND FRESH RASPBERRIES

This cake is another celebration of one of my favourite flavour combinations: lemon and raspberry. The decoration can be a bit tricky. It is inspired by the famous concorde cake, decorated with meringue cylinders. I would suggest that, after crumb coating with mascarpone frosting, you set the cake in the fridge then decorate with the meringue cylinders and raspberries just before serving. The meringue cylinders will be crisp when you decorate with them, but over time they will lose their crisp texture and became a bit like marshmallow, which is also delicious with this cake.

Serves ✿ 10–12

Bake 🍮 1½–2 hours

Ingredients

For the lemon genoise

8 medium free-range eggs
250g (9oz) caster sugar
2 teaspoons vanilla paste
zest of 2 lemons
250g (9oz) plain flour
75g (2¾oz) salted butter, melted,
 plus extra for greasing

For the French meringue cylinders

3 medium free-range egg whites
150g (5½oz) caster sugar

For the filling

1 batch Raspberry Curd (page 63),
 made with lemon juice rather
 than yuzu)

For assembly and decoration

1 batch Mascarpone Frosting
 (page 37)
400g (14oz) fresh raspberries

Method

To make the lemon genoise

1   Preheat the oven to 190°C/170°C fan/375°F/gas mark 5. Grease four 20cm (8in) cake tins with butter and line with baking paper.

2   In a large mixing bowl, whisk together the eggs and sugar using an electric whisk for about 10 minutes until the mixture has tripled in volume and reached the ribbon stage (see page 15).

3   Add the vanilla and lemon zest, then sift the flour over the batter. Gently but quickly fold in, taking care not to knock too much air out of the mixture.

4   Take a couple of tablespoons of the batter and mix with the melted butter in a separate bowl. Once combined, slowly pour the butter mixture into the batter and fold in.

5   Carefully divide the batter between the prepared tins and bake for 14–16 minutes until the batter starts to shrink away from the sides of the tins.

6   Remove from the oven and let the sponges cool in their tins for 10 minutes before turning out on to a wire rack to cool completely.

To make the French meringue cylinders

7   Reduce oven temperature to 110°C/90°C/225°F/gas mark ¼. Grease two baking trays and line with baking paper.

8   In a large, clean bowl, whisk the egg whites with an electric whisk until the mixture starts to form soft peaks. Now start adding the sugar, a tablespoon at a time, whisking well between each addition to make sure all the sugar is dissolved into the egg whites. Once all the sugar is incorporated, you should end up with a nice, glossy meringue.

9   Spoon the mixture into a piping bag fitted with a 1cm (½in) plain nozzle.

10 Pipe straight lines, 11–12cm (4¼–4½in) long, onto the prepared trays. Bake for 50–60 minutes, then turn the oven off. Leave the meringues to cool completely in the oven, with the door ajar.

RECIPE CONTINUES NEXT PAGE ▇▶

Everyday cakes – fully frosted cakes

To assemble and decorate

11 Use a little of the Macarpone Frosting to secure one of the sponges on a 25–30cm (10–12in) cake board or cake stand and place on a cake turntable.

12 Put half of the Macarpone Frosting in a piping bag and leave the rest in the bowl. Cut a 1cm (½in) opening in the end of the piping bag and pipe a circular border of Macarpone Frosting around the top of the sponge. Fill the inside of the ring with Raspberry Curd and a few raspberries, then top with another sponge. Repeat twice more until all the sponges are stacked.

13 Coat the sides and top of the cake with the rest of the Macarpone Frosting from the bowl. Place in the fridge to chill for 30 minutes.

14 Once set take the cake out of the fridge and use the cooled meringue cylinders to decorate the sides of the cake, then decorate the top with the remaining fresh raspberries and a drizzle of Raspberry Curd, if there is any left over.

15 The cake will keep in the fridge for couple of days, but the meringue will start to get soft and marshmallow-like

Chocolate genoise

WITH CHERRIES, CHERRY CREAM AND CHOCOLATE AND CHERRY GANACHE

This is the first, and simpler, of two chocolate and cherry cakes in this book. The recipe might look a bit boozy, but the addition of alcohol is optional. Two chocolate genoises are sandwiched with a thick layer of cream, cherry compote and sour cherries. The whole cake is covered with ganache and then coated with chocolate shavings. If cherries are in season decorate the top with some fresh cherries along with some left-over ganache kisses. But it would be as delicious without the fresh cherry decoration as well.

Serves ✿ 8–10

Bake 🍃 20–25 minutes

Ingredients

For the chocolate genoise

6 large free-range eggs
185g (6½oz) caster sugar
150g (5½oz) self-raising flour
50g (1¾oz) cocoa powder
60g (2¼oz) salted butter,
   melted, plus extra for greasing
1 teaspoon vanilla bean paste

For the cherry cream filling

250ml (9fl oz) double cream
1 tablespoon cherry brandy (optional)
2–3 tablespoons Cherry Compote
   (page 58)

For the chocolate and cherry ganache

250ml (9fl oz) double cream
250g (9oz) dark chocolate, chopped
2 teaspoons cherry brandy (optional)

For assembly and decoration

100g (3½oz) frozen sour cherries
150ml (5½fl oz) chocolate shavings
150ml (5½fl oz) whipping cream,
   whipped
150g (5½oz) melted chocolate
14–18 fresh cherries with stalks

Method

To make the chocolate genoise

1   Preheat the oven to 190°C/170°C fan/375°F/gas mark 5. Grease two 20cm (8in) cake tins with butter and line with baking paper.

2   In a large mixing bowl, whisk together the eggs and caster sugar with an electric whisk for about 10 minutes until the mixture has tripled in volume and reached the ribbon stage (page 15).

3   Sift the flour and cocoa powder over the batter and use a silicone spatula or metal spoon to carefully but swiftly fold them in without knocking too much air out of the batter. You may find it easier to add them in two batches.

4   Take a few tablespoons of the batter and mix thoroughly with the melted butter and vanilla bean paste in a separate bowl. Slowly drizzle the butter mixture over the batter and fold it in.

5   Divide the batter equally between the prepared tins and bake for 20–25 minutes, or until a skewer inserted into the middle comes out clean.

6   Remove from the oven and let the sponges cool in their tins for 5–10 minutes before turning out on to a wire rack to cool completely.

To make the cherry cream filling

7   In a mixing bowl, whisk together the cream and cherry brandy with an electric whisk until it forms soft peaks.

8   Divide the cream in half, then fold 2–3 tablespoons of Cherry Compote into one half. Keep chilled.

To make the chocolate and cherry ganache

9   Warm the cream in a saucepan over a medium heat until it is just about to boil. Pour the warm cream over the chocolate and set aside for 5 minutes.

10 Add the cherry brandy and mix together thoroughly until well combined.

RECIPE CONTINUES NEXT PAGE ➡️

Tip

Some freezer space will be handy while making this cake. After the crumb coat chill the cake preferably in the freezer to make sure the ganache and the cream filling set properly before covering the sides with chocolate shavings.

11   Pour one-third of the ganache into a bowl and cover with clingfilm. Let it cool to room temperature then fold the remaining half of the cherry cream (without the compote) into it. Spoon into a piping bag and set aside in the fridge.

12   Cover the remaining ganache with clingfilm, making sure the clingfilm is touching the surface of the ganache. Place in the fridge to chill for 30–60 minutes. Once the ganache is cooled and almost set, whisk using an electric whisk until it is lighter in colour and spreadable. Be careful not to over-whisk, or it will split. Spoon half the ganache into a piping bag and leave the rest in the bowl.

To assemble and decorate

13   Use a little ganache to secure one of the sponges on a 25–30cm (10–12in) cake board or cake stand and place on a cake turntable.

14   Cut a 1cm (½in) opening in the end of the piping bag of ganache with cream and pipe a circular border of ganache around the top of the sponge. Fill the circle with the cherry cream mixed with Cherry Compote, then push the sour cherries into the cream. Place the second sponge on top.

15   Coat the top and sides of the cake with the ganache from the bowl and place in the fridge to set for 30 minutes.

16   Once all set, serve. Once set, remove from the fridge and cover the sides of the cake with chocolate shavings.

17   Pipe some kisses of ganache with cream from the piping bag all over the top surface of the cake. Place some fresh cherries in between the kisses. Return the cake to fridge for another 30 minutes–1 hour.

18   The cake will keep in the fridge for a day, though as it contains so much fresh cream, I wouldn't suggest leaving it at room temperature for too long.

Raspberry and cream Swiss roll

The next three recipes are my favourite Swiss rolls. Obviously in a Swiss roll you always want to have a beautiful swirl. It is not difficult to get it right, just remember a few key things as you do it. You need to roll the Swiss roll when it is still warm and cover it with a tea towel to make sure the sponge doesn't dry out as it cools to room temperature. When it is cooled completely, carefully unroll and fill it with your filling. It is important to leave about 1–1.5cm (⅜–½in) from the edge as you spread the filling on the sponge. As you roll, the filling will reach the sides and cover the whole area of the sponge. For this raspberry ripple Swiss roll, I use a vanilla sponge rolled with a cream rippled with raspberry jam. The decoration is simple but effective with fresh raspberries. As you take it out to your friends and family everyone will be wowed just by the sight of it.

Serves ✿ 8–10

Bake 20–25 minutes

Ingredients

For the vanilla sponge

butter, for greasing
3 large free-range eggs
1 teaspoon vanilla bean paste
90g (3¼oz) caster sugar,
  plus extra for dusting
80g (2¾oz) plain flour

For the raspberry jam

1 batch Raspberry Jam (page 60)

For the cream filling

100g (3½oz) clotted cream
200ml (7fl oz) double cream
1½ teaspoons vanilla bean paste

For decoration

400g (14oz) fresh raspberries

Method

To make the vanilla sponge

1   Preheat the oven to 190°C/170°C fan/375°F/gas mark 5. Grease a Swiss roll tin and line with baking paper.

2   In a mixing bowl, whisk together the eggs, vanilla and sugar using an electric whisk for 5–7 minutes until tripled in volume and reached ribbon stage (page 15).

3   Sift the flour on top, then fold it in using a spatula or metal spoon, working gently but swiftly to avoid knocking too much air out of the batter.

4   Spoon the batter into the prepared tin and spread out using a spatula. Bake for 9–10 minutes until lightly golden.

5   Remove from the oven and let the cake cool slightly in the tin for 5 minutes. Lightly dampen a clean tea towel by spraying it with water. Place the tea towel on the work surface, and position a piece of baking paper slightly larger than the tin on top of the towel. Dust the baking paper with some caster sugar.

6   Carefully flip the Swiss roll tin on top of the baking paper, then remove the tin and carefully peel the lining baking paper from the bottom of the sponge.

7   With the help of the dampened tea towel, slowly start to roll the sponge inside the fresh sheet of baking paper, starting at the short end. Once rolled completely, let it cool.

RECIPE CONTINUES NEXT PAGE ▶▶

To make the cream filling

8   In a large bowl, whisk the clotted cream with the double cream and vanilla using a balloon whisk until you have stiff peaks. Don't over-whisk.

9   Transfer half the cream to a second bowl and fold in 2–3 tablespoons of the cooled Raspberry Jam to create a rippled cream. Place both bowls of cream in the fridge until needed.

To assemble and decorate

10   Unroll the sponge and then spread all the rippled cream over the surface. Drizzle rest of the jam on top.

11   With the help of the baking paper on the outside of the sponge, roll up the sponge tightly. Cover the Swiss roll with the tea towel and place in the fridge for 30 minutes to 1 hour to set.

12   Once set, remove from the fridge and remove the tea towel and baking paper. Cut both ends of the Swiss roll to reveal the spiral.

13   Use the non-rippled cream to coat the outside of the sponge.

14   Arrange the raspberries on the Swiss roll as shown in the photo.

15   The roll can be kept in the fridge for about a day.

Mango and cardamom Swiss roll

During my childhood summers in India confectioners used to make a special mishti called 'aamsotto Sandesh roll', one of my absolute favourite sweets. It is basically a little cylinder of sweetened cardamom flavoured ricotta, rolled in mango 'leather'. This Swiss roll is my tribute to that mishti. The cardamom-flavoured sponge is rolled with cardamom pastry crème and mango gelée. Just like the mishti, the whole Swiss roll is then also wrapped in mango gelée. It might be a bit difficult as you roll this sponge, but you have to be confident and do it. I hope you enjoy this translation of my favourite childhood sweet to a Swiss roll.

Serves ✿ 8–10

Bake 🧤 25–35 minutes

Ingredients

For the sponge

butter, for greasing
3 medium free-range eggs
90g (3¼oz) caster sugar,
    plus extra for dusting
80g (2¾oz) plain flour
1½ teaspoons ground cardamom

For the mango gelée

4 platinum-grade gelatine leaves
350g (12oz) mango purée
50g (1¾oz) water
50g (1¾oz) caster sugar

For the cardamom pastry crème

250ml (9floz)
1 teaspoon vanilla bean paste
2 teaspoons ground cardamom
3 medium free-range egg yolks
20g (¾oz) cornflour
40g (1½oz) caster sugar
75g (2¾oz) cold unsalted
    butter, cubed

For assembly and decoration

1 fresh mango, peeled and diced

Method

To make the sponge

1   Preheat the oven to 190°C/170°C fan/375°F/gas mark 5. Grease a Swiss roll tin with butter and line with baking paper.

2   In a large mixing bowl, whisk together the eggs and sugar using an electric whisk for about 5–7 minutes until it has tripled in volume and reached the ribbon stage (page 15).

3   Sift the flour and ground cardamom over the egg mix, then use a metal spoon or silicone spatula to gently but quickly fold them in without knocking too much air out of the batter.

4   Spoon the batter into the prepared baking tin and level the surface using a palette knife. Bake for 9–10 minutes until golden.

5   Remove from the oven and let the cake cool slightly in the tin for 5 minutes. Lightly dampen a clean tea towel by spraying it with water. Place the tea towel on the work surface, and position a piece of baking paper slightly larger than the tin on top of the towel. Dust the baking paper with some caster sugar.

6   Carefully invert the Swiss roll tin on top of the baking paper, then remove the tin and carefully peel the lining baking paper from the bottom of the sponge.

7   With the help of the dampened tea towel, slowly start to roll the sponge inside the fresh sheet of baking paper, starting at the short end. Once rolled completely, let it cool.

To make the mango gelée

8   Line two Swiss roll tins with clingfilm.

9   Soak the gelatine leaves in cold water for 5 minutes.

10 Meanwhile, warm the mango purée, water and sugar in a saucepan over a medium heat for 4–5 minutes, but don't boil. Take off the heat.

RECIPE CONTINUES NEXT PAGE ▶▶

11 Squeeze the excess water out of the gelatine leaves and add them to the mango mix. Whisk to dissolve the gelatine.

12 Divide the mango mixture equally between the prepared tins, then place in the freezer for 1–1½ hours to set completely.

To make the cardamom pastry crème

13 Make the cardamom pastry crème following the instructions on page 40, but using the quantities here.

To assemble and decorate

14 Once everything is cooled and the gelée is set, you can assemble the Swiss roll. Remember to whisk the pastry crème before you begin to make it spreadable.

15 Unroll the sponge and spread 2–3 tablespoons of the pastry crème over it. Carefully lift one sheet of mango gelée and place it on top. Then spread with another few tablespoons of pastry crème.

16 Use the baking paper, now on the outside of the sponge, to help you roll up the Swiss roll, gently but tightly. Place in the freezer to set for about 30 minutes.

17 Once set, coat the Swiss roll with some of the remaining pastry crème, then roll it inside the second sheet of mango gelée.

18 Decorate the top of the Swiss roll with some mango cubes. Serve straightaway or after chilling the roll in the fridge for 30 minutes.

19 This can be stored in the fridge for a day or two.

Chocolate, cardamom and caramel Swiss roll

Serves ✿ 8–10

Bake 🥄 10–12 minutes

Ingredients

For the chocolate and cardamom Swiss roll

Butter for greasing
4 medium free-range eggs
125g (4½oz) caster sugar
Salt
60g (2¼oz) plain flour
1 teaspoon ground cardamom
40g (1½oz) coco powder
20g (½oz) instant espresso
2 tablespoons icing sugar

For the caramel and cardamom filling

1 batch Caramel Cream Cheese
  Frosting (page 39)
1 teaspoom ground cardamom

For assembly and decoration

2 tablespoons cocoa powder
1 tablespoon instant espresso powder

Method

To make the chocolate and cardamom Swiss roll

1   Preheat the oven to 180°C/160°C fan/350°F/gas mark 4. Grease a Swiss roll tin with butter and line with baking paper.

2   In a large mixing bowl, whisk the eggs, sugar and salt using an electric whisk for 7–8 minutes or until the mixture is tripled in volume and reached the ribbon stage (page 15).

3   Divide the whisked egg mix in half. In one half, gently fold in the plain flour and ground cardamom using a spatula or large metal spoon. Be careful not to knock out too much air from the batter. Put the batter in a piping bag and set aside.

4   In the other half of the whisked egg mix, fold in instant espresso and the coco powder. Place this batter in a separate piping bag.

5   Cut the ends of both the piping bags to create openings of about 1cm (½in) and pipe straight lines of alternating batter diagonally across of the tin.

6   Bake the sponge in the preheated oven for 9–11 minutes, until it is springy to the touch, or a skewer inserted comes out clean.

7   Cut a piece of baking paper slightly larger than the tin and dust it liberally with icing sugar. Flip the sponge on the top of the icing-sugared baking paper and peel the lining paper off.

8   Place another piece of baking paper on top and flip the sponge again, as you want the sugared side to be inside the Swiss roll. Place a damp tea towel on top of the baking paper.

9   Roll the sponge and baking paper from the short end of the sponge, with the help of the tea towel, and let it cool completely.

To make the caramel and cardamom filling

10   Whisk Caramel Cream Cheese Frosting with ground cardamom and set aside in the fridge to be used later.

To assemble and decorate

11   To assemble, unroll the sponge and remove the top sheet of baking paper. Spread the filling evenly leaving a 1–1.5cm (⅜–½in) border around the edges. Roll it back again tightly with the help of the baking paper beneath. Cover it with the tea towel.

12   Chill the filled roll in the fridge for 30–45 minutes for the fillings to set.

13   Once set, take out of the fridge, remove the tea towel cover and serve.

14   It can be kept, covered, in the fridge for a couple of days but is best eaten within a day.

4

DECORATED CAKES

This chapter is all about my favourite cake-decorating trends. Personally, I don't think there should be any set rules: decorate how you think it looks pleasing and, most of all, enjoy the process.

The decorated cakes in this chapter may look more challenging than the cakes in the previous chapter, but they are not. If you can frost a cake, you can transform it into a drip cake with the addition of chocolate or caramel drips. After the drip cakes, there are three fault-line cakes. Parts of these cakes are decorated with something fun; it could be representative of the filling or flavour of the cake, or it could be hundreds and thousands or sprinkles. Then the cake is coated with a final layer of frosting on top of the fun decorative layer. As a result, it looks dramatic with the fun layer peeking through the 'faulty' smooth frosting. The first fault-line cake is a lemon-flavoured one, with a fun layer of lemon slices. The second is a rhubarb and ginger cake, hence it is decorated with rhubarb slices. This particular cake is inspired by Henry, who did the New Year *Bake Off* with me. He decorated his lemon and raspberry cake with roasted rhubarb slices. The decoration was so effective I couldn't resist trying it myself by turning it into a fault-line cake. Then comes the rainbow cake. Gorgeous layers of rainbow-coloured sponge are sandwiched with buttercream and covered with buttercream raffles.

The rainbow cake is followed first by a terrazzo cake and then one of the most popular cake trends ever, the geode cake. One of my favourite frostings is cookies and cream frosting. I used this to coat the piñata cake, it is simple and elegant with the rainbow kisses on top. The beauty of this cake is literally in the inside. As you cut it open, the contents cascade down like a river. I used Smarties, but you can use other sweets or candies or, for a healthier option, blueberries or chocolate-coated hazelnuts to fill the cavity inside.

The final three cakes in this chapter are chocolate collar cakes. The first is a milk chocolate cake sandwiched with white chocolate ganache and decorated with a dark chocolate collar and a chocolate sculpture. I kept this cake simple, with only a touch of gold in places. The chocolate collar in this cake could not be simpler. You basically take a piece of baking paper the same size as the sides of the cake. Scrunch the paper up and then flatten it again. Pour tempered chocolate on the paper and spread evenly before wrapping the cake with it. This might sound challenging, but it is a lot easier than you think. The second cake is a passion fruit cake with a chocolate mirror glaze and a lace chocolate collar. For this collar you pipe a lace pattern; it can be Jackson Pollock style or something very precise. The cardamom and kirsch Black Forest gateau, is a perfect cake to sum up this chapter. It has both a chocolate drip and a chocolate collar. This collar is made with tempered chocolate pieces that resemble bark. A bit different and more adaptable than the other two. But be experimental and feel free to mix and match different flavour combinations, frostings and decoration styles according to your preference.

Light fruit cake

WITH MARZIPAN FRUIT AND FLOWERS

Growing up in India, the only cake we had was for Christmas Day. There weren't too many choices either; there was only fruit cake. However, this fruit cake was very different to the boozy, fruit-heavy cake eaten in the UK during Christmas. It was more like a dense sponge cake with a handful of dried mixed fruit dispersed evenly in the crumb. I will be honest: I liked this cake a lot more than the British version. So here is my attempt to recreate my childhood fruit cake, except for the decoration: there was no trace of marzipan anywhere near it. I didn't even know what marzipan was before arriving in the UK. Anyway, as I love marzipan, why not combine my childhood cake memory with the flavours of my grown-up years? Hence this light fruit cake is covered and decorated with marzipan and the option of royal icing.

Serves ✿ 10–12

Bake 🍴 40–50 minutes

Ingredients

For the fruit

zest and juice of 2 oranges
50ml (2fl oz) brandy
350g (12oz) mixed dried fruit
2 tablespoons plain (all-purpose) flour

For the fruit cake

250g (9oz) unsalted butter, plus extra for greasing
5 medium free-range eggs
250g (9oz) dark muscovado sugar
225g (8oz) self-raising (self-rising) flour
1 teaspoon baking powder
75g (2¾oz) ground almonds
2 teaspoons ground cinnamon
2 teaspoons ground ginger
zest of 2 oranges

For assembly and decoration

1½ batches Marzipan (page 67)
yellow, red, green and blue gel food colouring
1 batch White Chocolate Ganache for Filling and Coating (page 55), flavoured with orange extract
2 tablespoons apricot jam
½ batch Royal Icing (page 70)

Method

To prepare the fruit

1   The day before you want to make the cake, you'll need to soak the fruit overnight. In a mixing bowl, combine the orange zest and juice with the brandy. Add the dried fruit, then cover and leave to soak overnight.

2   The next morning, sprinkle the flour over the soaked fruit and toss to coat.

To make the fruit cake

3   Preheat the oven to 180°C/160°C fan/350°F/gas mark 4. Grease two 20cm (8in) loose-bottomed baking tins with butter and line with baking paper.

4   Place all the ingredients except the soaked fruit in a mixing bowl and use an electric whisk to whisk them together for 1 minute. Scrape down the sides of the bowl and then whisk for a further minute.

5   Scatter the soaked fruit on top of the batter, then carefully fold in.

6   Divide the mixture equally between the prepared tins and bake for 35–40 minutes, or until a skewer inserted into the middle comes out clean.

7   Remove the cakes from the oven and leave to cool in the tin for 5–10 minutes, then transfer to a wire rack to cool completely.

To make the marzipan decorations

8   Take the half batch of marzipan and divide it into four portions. Keep one plain and add yellow, green and red food colouring to other three. Knead well to combine.

9   Create flowers with the coloured marzipan to be used for decoration (see page 68).

To prepare the whipped white chocolate ganache

10   Prepare the ganache according to the instructions on page 55, adding orange extract. Once the ganache is almost set, remove it from the fridge and whisk using an electric whisk until smooth and spreadable. Fill a piping bag with one-third of the whisked ganache and leave the rest in the bowl.

To assemble and decorate

11   Use a little ganache to secure one of the cakes on a 25–30cm (10–12in) cake board or cake stand and place on a cake turntable.

12   Cut a 1cm (½in) opening in the end of the piping bag and pipe a circular border of ganache around the top of the cake. Fill the inside of the ganache ring with the apricot jam.

13   Place the second cake on top. Coat the sides and top of the stacked cakes with a layer of ganache from the bowl and place in the freezer for 15 minutes to set.

14   Remove from the freezer and give the cake a final coat of ganache, smoothing the sides and top to give it a clear, clean edge. Return the cake to the fridge for 30 minutes to set completely.

15   Roll out the full batch of marzipan between two sheets of baking paper to create a 40cm (12in) circle. Remove the top layer of baking paper and carefully roll the marzipan on to the rolling pin.

16   Remove the cake from the fridge. Gently but quickly, bring the rolling pin close to one edge of the cake, and carefully unroll the marzipan on top. Use two fondant smoothers to smooth the marzipan over the top and sides of the cake. Trim the excess marzipan and set aside to be used to make flowers and leaves.

17   Crimp the marzipan around the top edge of the cake to create a decorative edge. Fill a piping bag with the royal icing and pipe some decorative designs around the cake.

18   Divide rest of the marzipan into 5 parts, Keep one white and colour the rest with the coloured food dye. Roll each coloured marzipan between two sheets of baking paper and stamp out different flower and leaves shapes as described in pages 68–69.

19   Finally, decorate with your marzipan flowers.

Chocolate, pear and ginger genoise
WITH CHOCOLATE GANACHE, CARAMEL SAUCE AND POACHED PEARS

I love the combination of chocolate and fruit, in particular pears. The fruity fragrance of pear perfectly complements the rich indulgence of dark and white chocolate. The best part of this cake is the poached pears assembled as a crown on top of the cake. You might think it is a bit crazy to add caramel to this heavenly combination, but somehow just a little caramel drip takes it to another level, both aesthetically and flavour-wise.

Serves ✿ 8–10

Bake ✤ 40–50 minutes

Ingredients

For the chocolate, pear and ginger genoise

3–4 knobs of stem ginger, chopped
2 Conference pears, peeled and chopped into small cubes
175g (5½oz) self-raising (self-rising) flour, plus 1 tablespoon for dusting
8 large free-range eggs
250g (6¾oz) dark brown sugar
75g (1¾oz) cocoa powder
60g (2¼oz) salted butter, melted, plus extra for greasing
1 teaspoon vanilla bean paste

For the poached pears

700ml (24fl oz) water
300g (10½oz) granulated sugar
4–5 green cardamom pods
2.5cm (1in) cinnamon stick
2 star anise
2 tablespoons freshly chopped ginger
7 medium Conference pears, peeled but stalks left on

For the chocolate ganache

1 batch Chocolate Ganache (page 49)

For the white chocolate buttercream

150g (5½oz) salted butter
150g (5½oz) icing sugar, sifted
150g (5½oz) white chocolate, melted and cooled

For assembly and decoration

4–5 tablespoons Caramel Sauce (page 44), to drizzle

Method

To make the chocolate, pear and ginger genoise

1   Preheat the oven to 190°C/170°C fan/375°F/gas mark 5. Grease three 15cm (6in) cake tins with butter and line with baking paper.

2   In a small bowl, combine the chopped ginger and pears. Scatter over the 1 tablespoon of flour and toss to coat, then set aside.

3   In a large mixing bowl, whisk together the eggs and sugar with an electric whisk for about 10 minutes until the mixture has tripled in volume and reached the ribbon stage (see page 15).

4   Sift the flour and cocoa powder over the batter and use a silicone spatula or metal spoon to carefully but swiftly fold them in without knocking too much air out of the batter. You may find it easier to add them in two batches.

5   Take a few tablespoons of the batter and mix thoroughly with the melted butter in a separate bowl. Slowly drizzle the butter mixture over the batter, then sprinkle in the flour-coated ginger and pears and gently fold to combine.

6   Divide the batter equally between the prepared tins and bake for 25–30 minutes, or until a skewer inserted into the middle comes out clean.

7   Remove the sponges from the oven and let them cool in their tins for 5–10 minutes before turning out on to a wire rack to cool.

To make the poached pears

8   Place the water, sugar and spices in a saucepan and bring to a simmer over a medium heat. Cut a small slice from the bottom of each pear so they can stand up when placed on top of the cake later.

9   Place the pears in the saucepan, laying them on their sides in the poaching liquid, cover and simmer for 15–25 minutes until they are soft but still holding their shape.

10 Remove the pears from the saucepan and leave to cool completely.

11 Once cool, chop two of the poached pears and leave the others whole.

To make the white chocolate buttercream

12 In a mixing bowl, whisk the butter using an electric whisk for about 5 minutes until it is light and fluffy. Add the icing sugar and whisk for a further 2–3 minutes.

13 Scrape down the sides of the bowl and whisk again, then add the cooled melted white chocolate. Whisk well for another 5 minutes until you have a nice, smooth consistency.

To assemble and decorate

14 Use a little ganache to secure one of the sponges on a 20cm (8in) cake board or cake stand and place on a cake turntable.

15 Cut a 1cm (½in) opening in the end of the piping bag with the ganache in and pipe a circular border of ganache around the top of the sponge. Fill the inside of the ring with half of the ganache mixed with the chopped poached pears.

16 Place the second sponge on top and repeat the step above, then top with the third sponge.

17 Coat the top and sides off the cake with a crumb coating of white chocolate buttercream, then place in the fridge to set for at least 30 minutes. Remove from the fridge and coat the sides of the cake with the remaining buttercream, smoothing it out with a palette knife or cake scraper.

18 Pour the caramel sauce on top of the cake and encourage it to drizzle down the sides.

19 Once the drip has set, decorate with the poached pears and serve.

20 This can be kept in the fridge for a couple of days, but remove the poached pears and save them separately in a tupperware container.

Orange and cardamom cake

WITH CHOCOLATE, ORANGE AND CARAMEL GANACHE, ORANGE ITALIAN MERINGUE BUTTERCREAM AND WHITE CHOCOLATE DRIP

I made this cake for some visitors at work. They loved the cake, and I loved the decoration. The white drizzle over the buttercream makes this cake looks like a candle.

Serves ✿ 6–8

Bake 🍴 30–45 minutes

Ingredients

For the orange and cardamom cake

100g (3½oz) hazelnuts
20g (¾oz) cornflour (cornstarch)
8 large free-range eggs
250g (9oz) caster (superfine) sugar
150g (5½oz) plain (all-purpose) flour
1½ tablespoons ground cardamom
zest of 3 large oranges
80g (2¾ oz) salted butter, melted and cooled, plus extra for greasing
juice of 2 large oranges
50g (1¾oz) caster sugar

For the chocolate, orange and caramel ganache

100g (3½oz) granulated sugar
zest of 2 oranges and juice of 1
70ml (2½fl oz) double (heavy) cream
100g (3½oz) dark chocolate, chopped
50g (1¾oz) chocolate and hazelnut spread
pinch of sea salt

For the orange Italian meringue buttercream

1 batch Italian Meringue Buttercream (page 33), flavoured with
2 teaspoons orange extract

For the white chocolate drip

75ml (2¾fl oz) double cream
100g (3½oz) white chocolate
orange food colouring gel

For assembly and decoration

oranges, clementines and satsumas
edible gold leaf (optional)

RECIPE CONTINUES NEXT PAGE ➡➡

Method

To make the orange and cardamom cake

1   Preheat the oven to 180°C/160°C fan/350°F/gas mark 4. Grease three 15cm (6in) cake tins with butter and line with baking paper.

2   Spread out the hazelnuts on a baking tray and roast for 10–15 minutes, then allow to cool.

3   Place the roasted hazelnuts in a food processor, along with the cornflour. Pulse to ground the nuts into coarse crumbs.

4   In a large mixing bowl, whisk together the eggs and sugar using an electric whisk for 7–10 minutes until the mixture has tripled in volume and reached the ribbon stage (page 15).

5   Sift the flour and cardamom over the batter, then add the ground hazelnuts. Gently fold everything together using a spatula or metal spoon. Add the orange zest and melted butter, and swiftly but carefully fold them in, taking care not to knock too much air out of the mixture.

6   Divide the batter equally between the prepared tins and bake for 35–40 minutes, or until a skewer inserted into the middle comes out clean.

7   Remove from the oven and let the sponges cool in their tins for 5–10 minutes before turning out on to a wire rack to cool completely.

8   Combine the orange juice with sugar in a small saucepan over a medium heat and bring to the boil. Let it boil for a few minutes, then take the pan off the heat and let the mixture cool to room temperature.

For the chocolate, orange and caramel ganache

9   Combine the sugar and the orange juice in a medium saucepan and place over a medium heat. Bring to the boil, but don't stir – let the sugar caramelise.

10 Meanwhile, warm the double cream in a separate saucepan over a medium heat.

11 Once the sugar is a dark amber colour, take both pans off the heat. Carefully whisk the double cream into the sugar and orange mixture.

12 Place the chocolate in a heatproof bowl and pour the hot caramel over the top. Wait a few minutes for the chocolate to melt then add the orange zest and salt, and whisk to combine. Finally, stir in the chocolate hazelnut spread.

13 Cover with clingfilm making sure the clingfilm is touching the surface of the ganache, and let it cool to room temperature.

To make the white chocolate drip

14 Warm the cream in a saucepan over a medium heat for 4–5 minutes, then pour it over the chopped white chocolate in a heatproof bowl. Wait a few minutes for the chocolate to melt then whisk in the food colouring to make it orange.

15 Spoon the drip mixture into a piping bag and set aside.

To assemble and decorate

16 Use a little of the buttercream to secure one of the sponges to a 20cm (8in) cake board on a cake turntable. Drizzle the sponge with a third of the orange syrup.

17 Put half the buttercream into a piping bag. Cut a 1cm (½in) opening in the end of the piping bag and pipe a circular border of buttercream around the top of the sponge, slowly rotating the turntable to help you. Fill the inside of the buttercream ring with half of the ganache, then place the second sponge on top.

18 Drizzle the second sponge with another third of the syrup, then repeat the step above with more buttercream and the rest of the ganache, before topping with the third sponge.

19 Soak the third sponge with the remaining syrup, then use half of the remaining buttercream to give the top and sides of the cake a crumb coating. Place it in the freezer for 30 minutes to set.

20 Remove the cake from the freezer and coat with the remaining buttercream, using a cake scraper or palette knife for a smooth finish. Return the cake to the freezer for 20–30 minutes to set.

21 Remove the cake from the freezer. Take the piping bag filled with white chocolate drip and cut a 3–4mm (⅒in) opening in the end. Pipe the drip along the edges of the cake, then pipe the rest on top of the cake and smooth it out using a palette knife.

22 Decorate the top of the cake with oranges, clementines, satsumas and their leaves. For a bit of optional bling, add a little edible gold leaf to the fruits.

Chocolate, orange and mint candy cane cake

I first made this cake as a present to the staff of Rotherham Leisure Complex. Since I moved to Rotherham in 2015, some of the staff have became close friends. Also, they got to taste a lot of pre-*Bake Off* cakes – it was like a weekly ritual. In a sense, it is my way of thanking them for becoming my friends and giving me company when I was new to Rotherham.

Serves ✿ 6–8

Bake ♥ 45–50 minutes

Ingredients

For the chocolate, orange and mint cake

120ml (4¼fl oz) boiling water
100g (3½oz) cocoa powder
zest and juice of 2 oranges
500g (1lb 2 oz) caster (superfine) sugar
200g (7oz) Greek yogurt
150g (5½oz) salted butter, at room temperature, plus extra for greasing
5 medium free-range eggs
300g (10½oz) self-raising flour
½ teaspoon baking powder
3 tablespoons finely chopped mint leaves (or 1½ tablespoons dried mint)
1 teaspoon peppermint extract

For the peppermint buttercream

250g (9oz) unsalted butter, at room temperature soft
475g icing (confectioner's) sugar (sifted)
1–2 tablespoons whole (full-fat) milk
1½ teaspoons peppermint extract
4–5 candy canes, crushed

For the peppermint drip

75ml (2¾fl oz) double (double) cream
100g (3½oz) white chocolate, chopped
red food colouring gel
½ teaspoon peppermint extract

Method

To make the chocolate, orange and mint cake

1   Preheat the oven to 180°C/160°C fan/350°F/gas mark 4. Grease three 15cm (6in) cake tins with butter and line with baking paper.

2   In a large mixing bowl, whisk together the boiling water, cocoa and orange zest and juice using an electric whisk until well combined. Scrape down the sides of the bowl and add the remaining cake ingredients, then whisk for about 1 minute. Scrape down the sides of the bowl once more and whisk for another 30 seconds.

3   Divide the batter equally between the prepared tins and bake for 45–50 minutes until a skewer inserted into the middle comes out clean.

4   Remove from the oven and let the cakes cool in their tins for 10–15 minutes before turning out on to a wire rack to cool completely.

To make the peppermint buttercream

5   In a mixing bowl, beat the butter using an electric whisk for about 5–10 minutes, scraping down the sides of the bowl from time to time. The colour of the butter should transform from yellow to pale cream as you keep whisking.

6   Sift in half of the icing sugar and mix very well for about 5 minutes, then scrape down the sides of the bowl and add the rest of the sugar. Whisk well for another 5 minutes.

7   Add 1–2 tablespoons of milk, depending on the consistency of the buttercream, and mix well, then add the peppermint extract and whisk to combine.

8   Remove about a third of the buttercream and place in a separate bowl, along with the crushed candy canes. Mix to combine: this will be the filling. The other two-thirds of the peppermint buttercream will be used for coating the cake.

RECIPE CONTINUES NEXT PAGE ➡➡

For assembly and decoration

2–3 red-and-white spiral lollipops
20–25 candy canes

To make the peppermint drip

9   Place the cream and white chocolate in a microwave-safe bowl and microwave on high power in 30-second bursts until the chocolate is melted. Add the red food colouring and mix well. Pour into a piping bag and set aside until needed.

To assemble and decorate

10   Use a little of the peppermint buttercream to secure one of the sponges on a 20cm (8in) cake board or cake stand and place on a cake turntable. Spread half the candy cane-filled buttercream on top, smoothing it out using a small spatula, then top with the second sponge. Spread this with the remaining candy cane-filled buttercream, then top with the third sponge.

11   Coat the sides and top of the cake with a crumb coating of the peppermint buttercream, then chill in the fridge for about an hour.

12   Remove the cake from the fridge and use the remaining buttercream to give it a final, smooth coating. Return the cake to the fridge for a further 30 minutes.

13   Cut 10–15 of the candy canes into small pieces and arrange them side by side around the base of the cake, pressing them into the icing.

14   Cut a 2–3mm ($\frac{1}{16}$–$\frac{1}{8}$in) hole in the end of the piping bag filled with the drip mixture and pipe some drips down the sides of the cake. Pour the rest of the drip mixture on top of the cake and smooth it out. Return the cake to the fridge for another 30 minutes to set.

15   Once set, remove the cake from the fridge and decorate the top with the remaining candy canes.

16   This can be kept in the fridge for a few days. While storing, take the candy canes off to save some space..

Lemon and fennel fault-line cake

WITH LEMON CURD AND LEMON SWISS MERINGUE BUTTERCREAM

This cake was for my colleague Iwona's pre-maternity cake. Both of us came for the interview at Nuclear AMRC on the same day. She loves lemon cake, so before she had her son, I made a lemon cake coated with white chocolate ganache and sugar flowers. This time I wanted to make something a little different and fun, hence this cake. It is simple but an ideal showstopping cake for any small gathering and parties.

Serves ✿ 7–8

Bake 👤 1 hour–1 hour 30 minutes

Ingredients

For the lemon and fennel cake

5 medium free-range eggs
250g (9oz) unsalted butter, at room
   temperature, plus extra for greasing
250g (9oz) caster (superfine) sugar
250g (9oz) self-raising (self-rising)
   flour
zest of 3 large lemons
1 tablespoon ground roasted
   fennel seeds

For the lemon and fennel syrup

juice of 4 lemons
100g (3½oz) caster sugar
1 tablespoon fennel seeds

For the filling

1 batch Lemon Curd (page 62)

Frosting

1–1½ batches Swiss Meringue
   Buttercream (page 34)
2 teaspoons lemon extract

For assembly and decoration

2–3 lemons, thinly sliced
2–3 whole lemons, with leaves
edible gold paint and edible gold
   beads

Method

To make the lemon and fennel cake

1   Preheat the oven to 180°C/160°C fan/350°F/gas mark 4. Grease three 15cm (6in) cake tins with butter and line with baking paper.

2   Place all the sponge ingredients in a large mixing bowl and whisk using an electric whisk for 1 minute until the batter is light and fluffy. Scrape down the sides of the bowl and whisk for 1 minute.

3   Divide the batter equally between the prepared tins. Bake for 45–50 minutes, or until a skewer inserted into the centre comes out clean.

4   Remove from the oven and let the cakes cool in their tins for 5–10 minutes, then turn them out on to a wire rack to cool completely.

To make the lemon and fennel syrup

5   Place all the syrup ingredients into a small saucepan over a medium heat and bring it to a boil. Take it off the heat and leave to cool to room temperature.

To make the frosting

6   Whisk the Swiss meringue buttercream with the lemon extract. Spoon the buttercream into a large piping bag and set aside.

To assemble and decorate

7   Place the lemon slices in a microwave-safe bowl and pour in enough water to cover them. Microwave on high for 30–45 seconds, then drain the water.

8   Lay the lemon slices on some kitchen paper and pat dry.

9   Once the sponges are cooled, you can assemble the cake. Use a little buttercream to secure one of the sponges on a 20cm (8in) cake board. Place the cake board on a cake turntable. Drizzle the sponge with a third of the lemon syrup.

10 Cut a 1cm (½in) opening in the end of the piping bag and pipe a circular border of buttercream around the top of the sponge, slowly rotating the turntable. Fill the inside of the buttercream ring with lemon curd and place the second sponge on the top.

RECIPE CONTINUES NEXT PAGE ➡➡

Decorated cakes – fault-line

The trick to getting the lemons to stick on the side of the cake is to slice them thinly. Then microwave them for 30–40 seconds in water and pat dry on kitchen paper (towel).This process makes them flexible and easy
to stick onto the buttercream.

11 Repeat the same process, drizzling the second sponge with another third of the syrup, then topping it with buttercream and lemon curd, before placing the third sponge on top. Drizzle the third sponge with the rest of the syrup.

12 Coat the sides and top of the cake with a crumb coating of buttercream to lock the loose crumbs in place. Place the cake in the fridge for 40 minutes (or in the freezer for 20 minutes) for the buttercream to set.

13 Remove the cake from the fridge or freezer and pipe a thin layer of buttercream around the middle layer of the cake, almost like a belt. Spread it using a palette knife.

14 Press the lemon slices on to this buttercream belt, trying to fit on as many slices as possible; you might have to cut a few in half. Transfer the cake to the freezer for 15 minutes to set.

15 Pipe thick layers of buttercream above and below the lemon layer. You want the buttercream layer to be thicker than the lemon layer, to give the impression that the lemon slices are inside the cake.

16 Use a cake scraper to carefully smooth out the sides of the cake, then return to the freezer for an hour to set completely.

17 Once set, remove the cake from the freezer and paint the open edges of the buttercream around the lemon layer, as well as the top of the cake, with edible gold paint and place a few gold beads along the edges.

18 Decorate with the whole lemons with leaves; you can halve some of them if you like.

19 The cake can be stored in the fridge for a couple of days, but the lemon slices will shrink over time and will not look as pretty.

Rhubarb, ginger and custard fault-line cake

This is my interpretation of rhubarb and custard in cake form. It is delicious and the rhubarb fault-line decoration make it looks very beautiful.

Serves ✿ 14–16

Bake 1 hour–1 hour 30 minutes

Ingredients

For the ginger cake

7–8 knobs of stem ginger, chopped
350g (12oz) self-raising (self-rising) flour,
    plus 1 tablespoon for dusting
7 medium free-range eggs
350g (12oz) caster (superfine) sugar
350g (12oz) unsalted butter, at room temperature, plus extra for greasing
1 teaspoon baking powder
3 teaspoons vanilla bean paste
3 teaspoons ground ginger

For the rhubarb and ginger compote

200g (7oz) rhubarb, diced
100g (3½oz) dark brown sugar
zest and juice of 1 lemon
2 teaspoons freshly chopped ginger
1 teaspoon chopped bird's eye chilli
    or ½ teaspoon dried chilli flakes
1 teaspoon crushed fennel seeds

For assembly and decoration

1 batch Vanilla and Cardamom Pastry Crème (variation, page 40)
1 batch Italian Meringue Buttercream (page 33)
10–15 rhubarb stems, sliced into thick strips, about 4–5cm (1½–2in) long and 3–4mm (⅛–¼in) wide and 2–3mm (1⁄16–⅛in) thick
edible rose gold paint

Method

To make the ginger cake

1. Preheat the oven to 170°C/150°C fan/340°F/gas mark 3½. Grease two deep 15cm (6in) cake tins and two deep 10cm (4in) cake tins with butter and line with baking paper.

2. Place the stem ginger pieces in a small bowl and dust over the 1 tablespoon flour. Toss to coat, then set aside.

3. In a large mixing bowl, whisk all the cake ingredients, except the stem ginger, with an electric whisk for a couple of minutes until light and fluffy. Scrape down the sides of the bowl and whisk for another minute.

4. Finally, fold in the stem ginger. Divide the mixture between the prepared tins, filling each one about two-thirds full. Bake the smaller cakes on the lower shelf of the oven (not on the oven floor) and the larger cakes in the middle shelf – this way they will take a similar time to bake – for 50–60 minutes or until a skewer inserted into the middle comes out clean.

5. Remove from the oven and let the cakes cool in their tins for 5–10 minutes before turning out on to a wire rack to cool completely.

To make the rhubarb and ginger compote

6. Combine all the ingredients in a saucepan over a medium heat. Bring to the boil, stirring occasionally, and cook until most of the liquid has evaporated and you have a nice spreadable compote. This will take 7–10 minutes.

To assemble and decorate

7. Spoon the pastry crème into a piping bag and set aside. Spoon three-quarters of the buttercream into a second piping bag and set aside, leaving the rest in the bowl.

8. Once the cakes are cool, slice each one horizontally so you have four 15cm (6in) sponge layers and four 10cm (4in) sponge layers.

9. Use a little buttercream to secure the first 15cm (6in) sponge layer on a 20cm (8in) cake board. Place the cake board on a cake turntable.

RECIPE CONTINUES NEXT PAGE ▶▶

10 Cut a 1cm (½in) opening in the end of the piping bag and pipe a circular border of pastry crème around the top of the sponge, slowly rotating the turntable. Fill the inside of the pastry crème ring with some of the rhubarb and ginger compote. Pipe and spread a thin layer of pastry crème on top of the jam, then place a second 15cm (6in) sponge layer on top.

11 Repeat this process to stack and sandwich the third and fourth 15cm (6in) sponge layers with pastry crème and compote.

12 Coat the sides and top of the cake with buttercream and smooth it using a palette knife or a cake scraper. Place the cake in the freezer for 30 minutes for the buttercream to set.

13 Repeat the steps above to stack, sandwich and coat the 10cm (4in) sponge layers on a 15cm (6in) cake board, then place in the freezer to set.

14 Once set, take the larger cake out of the freezer and pipe a thin layer of buttercream around the top 4–5cm (1½–2in) of the cake. Spread using a palette knife, then stick some rhubarb slices to the buttercream, going all the way around. Return to the freezer to set.

15 For the smaller cake, spread a thin layer of buttercream around the bottom 4–5cm (1½–2in) of the cake. Stick the remaining rhubarb slices to the buttercream, going all the way around, and return the cake to the freezer.

16 When the rhubarb slices are set on the buttercream, take the larger cake out of the freezer and pipe a thick layer of buttercream around the bottom part of the cake. Make sure that the bottom ends of the rhubarb slices are covered with buttercream. It should look as if the rhubarb slices are reaching down the whole length of the cake under the buttercream. Smooth the buttercream with a cake scraper and return to the freezer for an hour.

17 Now pipe a thick layer of buttercream around the top part of the smaller cake, making sure the top ends of the rhubarb slices are hidden by the buttercream. Return to the freezer to set for an hour.

18 To stack the tiers of the cake, you'll need to use about four wooden or plastic dowels. Carefully insert the first dowel inside the larger cake. Mark the place where the dowel meets the top of the cake with an edible marker. Take the dowel out and cut to size using a knife or scissors. Repeat for the rest of the dowels.

19 Insert the dowels into the cake at the corners of an imaginary 8cm (3¼in) square in the middle.

20 Spread a thin layer of buttercream on top of the larger cake, then place the smaller cake on top, positioning it over the dowels.

21 Finally, paint the open edges of the buttercream around the rhubarb slices and the top of the cake with the edible rose gold paint.

Coconut, lime and raspberry fault-line cake

Serves ✿ **7–8**

Bake ✋ 1 hour–1 hour 15 minutes

Ingredients

For the coconut and lime cake

300g (10½oz) unsalted butter,
   at room temperature, plus extra
   for greasing
300g (10½oz) caster (superfine)
   sugar
6 medium free-range eggs
250g (9oz) self-raising (self-rising)
   flour
100g (3½oz) desiccated (shredded)
   coconut, toasted
2 teaspoons ground cardamom
zest of 3 limes

For the lime drizzle

juice of 4 limes
75g (2¾oz) caster sugar

For the raspberry curd with
fresh raspberries

1 batch Raspberry Curd (page 63)
100g (3½oz) fresh raspberries
zest of 1 lime

For the candy-melt decoration
and stripes

100–150g (3½–5½oz) each of white,
   green and red candy melts

For assembly and decoration

1 batch Swiss meringue buttercream
(page 34)
250g (9oz) fresh raspberries
50g coconut flakes, toasted

Method

To make the coconut and lime cake

1   Preheat the oven to 180°C/160°C fan/350°F/gas mark 4.
    Grease three 15cm (6in) cake tins with butter and
    line with baking paper.

2   In a large mixing bowl, whisk together all the cake ingredients
    using an electric whisk for about 1 minute until light and fluffy.

3   Scrape down the sides of the bowl and whisk for another minute,
    then divide the batter equally between the prepared tins.

4   Bake for 40–50 minutes, or until a skewer inserted into the
    middle comes out clean.

5   Remove from the oven and let the cakes cool in their tins
    for 5–10 minutes before turning out on to a wire rack
    to cool completely.

To make the lime drizzle

6   Combine the lime juice and sugar in a saucepan over a medium
    heat and bring to the boil. Boil for a few minutes, then take it off
    the heat and leave to cool to room temperature.

To make the raspberry curd with fresh raspberries

7   Place the raspberry curd in a bowl, then fold in the fresh
    raspberries and lime zest.

To assemble and decorate

8   Use a little of the buttercream to secure the first sponge
    on to a 20cm (xin) cake board on a cake turntable. Drizzle
    the sponge with a third of the lime syrup.

9   Put half the buttercream into a piping bag. Cut a 1cm (xin)
    opening in the end of the piping bag and pipe a circular border
    of buttercream around the top of the first sponge, slowly rotating
    the turntable to help you. Fill the inside of the buttercream ring
    with half of the raspberry curd, then place the second sponge
    on top.

10 Drizzle the second sponge with another third of the syrup, then
    repeat the step above with more buttercream and the rest
    of the raspberry curd, before topping with the third sponge.

11 Soak the third sponge with the remaining syrup, then coat the
    sides and top of the cake with a crumb coating of buttercream.
    Place the cake in the fridge for 30–45 minutes for the
    buttercream to set.

RECIPE CONTINUES NEXT PAGE ▶▶

12 Remove the cake from the fridge and pipe a thin layer of buttercream around the middle layer of the cake, almost like a belt. Spread it using a palette knife.

13 In three separate bowls, melt each colour of candy melts in the microwave on high power in around three 30-second bursts. Then transfer into three piping bags. Measure the perimeter of the cake and lay out an acetate strip 6-7cm wide and with the length of the perimeter of the cake. Pipe stripes of melted candy melts on to the acetate strips, using the other half from the piping bags, alternating red, green and white. Leave to set slightly, then carefully lift the acetate strips and stick them to the sides of the cake in the middle. Return the cake to the fridge to set completely for about 15–20 minutes.

14 Once set, remove the cake from the fridge and carefully unwrap the acetate. The candy-melt stripes should now be attached to the cake.

15 Pipe thick layers of buttercream above and below the candy-melt stripes. You want the buttercream layer to be thicker than the stripy layer, to give the impression that the coloured stripes are inside the cake.

16 Use a cake scraper to carefully smooth out the sides of the cake, then place it in the freezer for an hour to set completely.

17 Once set, remove from the freezer and decorate the top edge of the cake with fresh raspberries arranged in a circle. Fill the inside of the circle with toasted coconut flakes. Keep the cake chilled, but remove from the fridge a couple of hours before serving.

18 It can be stored in the fridge for up to couple of days.

Rainbow cake

WITH RAINBOW RUFFLES

Serves ✿ 12–16

Bake 🖤 1 hour–1 hour 30 minutes

Ingredients

For the rainbow cake

750g (1lb 10oz) unsalted butter,
  plus extra for greasing
750g (1lb 10oz) caster (superfine)
  sugar
zest of 6 lemons
2 teaspoons vanilla bean paste
9 large free-range eggs
750g (1lb 10oz) self-raising flour
6 tablespoons whole (full-fat) milk
6 tablespoons Greek yogurt
red, orange, yellow, green, blue
  and purple food colouring gel

For assembly and decoration

2½–3 batches of Swiss Meringue
  Buttercream (page 34)

Method

To make the rainbow cake

1   Preheat the oven to 180°C/160°C fan/350°F/gas mark 4. Grease six 20cm (8in) tins with butter and line with baking paper. (If you don't have six baking tins, then you can bake in batches.)

2   As there is so much batter to mix here, it's easiest to prepare this in a stand mixer. (Again, you might prefer to bake in batches if you don't have a stand mixer; the ingredients are easy to divide into three batches.)

3   Cream the butter and sugar together using an electric whisk or the beater attachment of your stand mixer for 10 minutes until light and fluffy.

4   Add the lemon zest and vanilla, along with the first egg, and whisk for 30 seconds until incorporated. Scrape down the sides of the bowl, then add the next egg and whisk again. Keep going until all the eggs are incorporated.

5   Next, sift in the flour and mix on the lowest speed to combine.

6   Take out six medium-sized bowls and add 1 tablespoon of milk and 1 tablespoon of yogurt to each bowl. Add a different colour to each one – red, orange, yellow, green, blue and purple – then whisk to combine.

7   Add a sixth of the batter to each of the bowls (about 450g (1lb) each) and carefully fold the colour into the cake batter, without knocking out too much air.

8   Pour each coloured batter into one of the prepared tins and bake for 23–25 minutes, or until a skewer inserted into the middle comes out clean.

9   Remove from the oven and let the cakes cool in their tins for 5–10 minutes before turning out on to a wire rack to cool completely.

To assemble and decorate

10 This recipe requires two and a half to three batches of Swiss meringue buttercream. Keep one batch white for sandwiching the sponges and crumb coating. Divide the other batch evenly between six different bowls. Colour each bowl with a different rainbow colour. It is better to use oil-based/soluble colours for colouring buttercream, as it provides a much more vivid colour.

11 If using gel colouring that is water soluble, mix the colours with a tablespoon of milk and whisk in the buttercream.

RECIPE CONTINUES NEXT PAGE ➡➡

12 Take a large piping bag and fit it with a petal nozzle. Spoon coloured buttercream into the piping bag. First spoon red, followed by orange, yellow green, blue and purple. So as you pipe you will get one colour and a natural transition of that colour to the next.

13 Use a little of the white buttercream to secure the purple sponge to a 25–30cm (10–12in) cake board or cake stand on a cake turntable. Spoon 2 tablespoons of white buttercream on top of the purple sponge and spread it out using a palette knife. Place the blue sponge on top.

14 Repeat the process above to sandwich and stack the coloured sponges with the white buttercream, so that the ascending order is purple, blue, green, yellow, orange and red.

15 Coat the sides and top of the cake with a crumb coating of white buttercream, then place it in the freezer to set for 1 hour.

16 Once the crumb coat has set, you can start piping the ruffles on the sides of the cake, in a vertical direction. Hold your piping bag at the base of the cake at a right angle and, with the wide part of the nozzle touching the surface of the cake, slowly squeeze the piping bag with constant pressure while slowly piping vertically upwards. You can slightly wiggle your piping bag as you are piping to make wavy ruffles, which looks pretty.

17 Keep going until you have covered the sides and top of the cake with rainbow-coloured ruffles. As you pipe, just make sure that the ruffles are close to each other so that you can't see the crumb-coat layer underneath. Place the cake in the fridge for a couple of hours to set completely.

18 Once set, bring it out in front of your friends and family. I can guarantee it will wow everyone. Let the cake come to room temperature before serving. This cake will keep a couple of days in the fridge, but take it out of the fridge few hours before serving.

Plum and almond cake

WITH TERRAZZO FROSTING

There are different ways to make terrazzo decoration. I found the easiest way is by using whipped white chocolate ganache which also gives a neater finish and sets faster than buttercream.

Serves ✿ 7–8

Bake 🍶 1 hour–1 hour 15 minutes

Ingredients

For the plum and almond cake

8 firm plums, stoned and diced into
   1cm (½in) chunks
325g (11½oz) self-raising (self-rising)
   flour, plus 1 tablespoons for dusting
400g (14oz) unsalted butter
400g (14oz) caster (superfine) sugar
8 medium free-range eggs
125g (4½oz) ground almonds
1 tablespoon ground cardamom
1 teaspoon baking powder
2 teaspoons almond extract

For the plum compote

8–10 firm plums, quartered
3 tablespoons dark brown sugar
1 teaspoon Bengali five spice, ground

For the terrazzo frosting

2 batches White Chocolate Ganache
   (page 55)
Red and maroon gel food colouring

For assembly and decoration

ripe plums

Method

To make the plum and almond cake

1   Preheat the oven to 180°C/160°C fan/350°F/gas mark 4. Grease four 20cm (8in) cake tins with butter and line with baking paper.

2   In a small bowl, toss the chopped plums in the 1 tablespoon of flour to coat, then set aside.

3   In a large mixing bowl, whisk together all the other ingredients with an electric whisk for about 1 minute until everything is well incorporated.

4   Scrape down the sides of the bowl, then add the flour-coated plums and fold to combine.

5   Divide the batter between the prepared tins and bake for 25–30 minutes, or until a skewer inserted into the middle comes out clean.

6   Remove from the oven and let the cakes cool in their tins for about 10 minutes before turning out on to a wire rack to cool completely.

To make the plum compote

7   Place the plums, sugar and five spice in a saucepan over a medium heat. Bring to the boil, stirring so the mixture does not stick to the bottom. Once the mixture is reduced by half, take it off the heat and leave to cool completely.

To make the terrazzo frosting

8   Prepare the white chocolate ganache as described on page 55. Once it is almost set, remove from the fridge and divide into two bowls. Take one bowl and whisk using an electric whisk until the ganache is nice and spreadable. Spoon it into a piping bag. This will be used to coat and sandwich the sponges.

9   Whisk the second bowl of ganache in the same way, but then remove one-third of it and divide this into two. Colour them with red and maroon food colouring.

10   Take out two small piping bags. Fill one with a few tablespoons of red ganache, another with a few tablespoons of the maroon ganache. These will be used for the terrazzo decorations.

RECIPE CONTINUES NEXT PAGE ▶▶

To assemble and decorate

11   Use a little of the white chocolate ganache to secure one of the sponges to a 25–30cm (10–12in) cake board or cake stand and place it on a cake turntable.

12   Take the first piping bag of white chocolate ganache and cut a 1cm (½in) opening in the end of bag. Pipe a circular border of ganache around the top of the sponge, slowly rotating the turntable to help you. Fill the inside of the ganache circle with a third of the plum compote, then top with the second sponge.

13   Repeat the step above twice more to sandwich all the sponges with ganache and plum compote, placing the fourth sponge on top.

14   Coat the top and sides of the cake with a crumb coating of ganache, then place it in the freezer for 30 minutes to set completely.

15   Remove the cake from the freezer and coat it with a thick layer of white ganache on the sides of the cake, smoothing it out with a cake scraper. Return to the freezer for another 30 minutes to set.

16   Once set, remove the cake from the freezer. Using the back of a spoon, or a palette knife with a tapered end, remove small chunks of ganache from the sides of the cake, creating little holes in the frosting. A total of 30–40 would look good for this size of cake.

17   Fill the insides of these holes with the red and maroon coloured ganache. After filling all the holes, use a cake scraper to smooth the sides of the cake again, then return it to the freezer for 15–20 minutes to set.

18   Decorate the cake with fresh whole and halved plums.

19   Once this cake is set, you can keep it outside for a day. After that, it is better to place in the fridge, but try to consume with couple of days.

Citrus Madeira cake

WITH CONCRETE FROSTING AND GEODE DECORATIONS

Here is another rock-inspired showstopping cake: the geode. This is dedicated to some of the bravest, strongest and happiest people I know. You might be tired, tormented and shattered from your everyday battle, but let your inner beauty shine and show the world that you are invincible! I made it for my friend Sue's 60th birthday in lockdown. She is one of the most colourful people I know. You wouldn't believe when you see her that she was battling cancer and after surgery she won! So, this cake is for you, Sue, and to all of the Sues out there who are being brave and are fighting their own battles with their colourful hearts.

Serves ✿ 8–10

Bake ❦ 1 hour 15 minutes–
1 hour 30 minutes

Ingredients

For the Madeira cake

600g (1lb 5 oz) caster (superfine) sugar
600g (1lb 5 oz) unsalted butter, at room temperature, plus extra for greasing
9 large free-range eggs
2 teaspoons vanilla extract
zest of 5 lemons
zest of 3 oranges
550g (1lb 4oz) self-raising (self-rising) flour
100g (3½oz) ground almonds
50ml (2fl oz) whole (full-fat) milk

For the concrete frosting

2 batches White Chocolate Ganache for Filling and Coating (page 55)
black and grey food colouring gel

For assembly and decoration

250g (9oz) orange, yellow, red and clear boiled sweets, crushed, or candy sugar crystals
red, yellow and orange food colouring gel

Method

To make the Madeira cake

1   Preheat the oven to 180°C/160°C fan/350°F/gas mark 4. Grease four 15cm (6in) cake tins with butter and line with baking paper.

2   In a large mixing bowl, whisk together the sugar and butter using an electric whisk for 7–10 minutes until light and fluffy, scraping down the sides of the bowl every now and then.

3   Add the eggs one at a time and whisk after each addition to make sure it is incorporated well before adding the next one.

4   After all the eggs are incorporated, stir in the vanilla and both types of citrus zest. Sift the flour over the batter, add the ground almonds and mix on the lowest speed to combine. Finally, scrape down the sides of the bowl and add the milk and mix well using a spatula or metal spoon.

5   Divide the mixture equally between the prepared baking tins. Bake for 45–50 minutes, or until a skewer inserted into the centre comes out clean.

6   Once baked, remove from the oven and let the cakes cool in their tins for 5–10 minutes before turning out on to a wire rack to cool completely.

To prepare the white chocolate ganache

7   Prepare the white chocolate ganache as described on page 55. Place both batches in the fridge to cool until almost set, then take one batch out of the fridge and whisk with an electric whisk until the ganache is light, fluffy and spreadable.

To assemble and decorate

8   Use a little of the whipped ganache to secure one of the sponges to a 20cm (8in) cake board or cake stand and place the cake board on a cake turntable.

RECIPE CONTINUES NEXT PAGE ➡➡

9   Spoon a couple of tablespoons of whipped ganache on top of the sponge and smooth with a palette knife while rotating the turntable.

10 Place the second sponge on top and repeat, then place the third sponge on top of that. Once all the sponges are stacked, coat the sides and top of the cake with the remaining whipped ganache and smooth the sides using a palette knife or cake scraper.

11 Transfer the cake to the freezer for 30 minutes for the ganache to set.

To make the concrete frosting

12 Now take the other bowl of white chocolate ganache out of the fridge. Whisk it for about 5 minutes until it becomes fluffy and spreadable.

13 Transfer one-third of the whipped ganache into a separate bowl an divide this in two parts. Mix black food colouring with one part and gray with the other.

14 Remove the cake from the freezer and coat generously with the white ganache. Smooth the sides using a pallet knife/cake scraper and place in the fridge to set. Next, use a palette knife to apply big blobs of grey ganache to the sides of the cake. In between the grey ganache blobs, apply a few smaller blobs of black ganache. Use a cake scraper to smooth it out completely. Next, use the side of the scraper to lightly mark some straight lines on the side of the cake, to give a realistic concrete look.

15 Place the cake in the fridge for 30–45 minutes to set the ganache.

To make the geode decoration

16 Cut out a triangular section from the top and side of the cake. It looks more realistic if the triangle is slightly imperfect or at an angle. Cover the inside of the cut-out section with ganache.

17 Starting from the centre, start sticking the crushed boiled sweets or candy sugar crystals on the cut-out section of the cake. The ganache will help them to stick. It looks better if you arrange them with darker colours towards the middle and lighter colours as you come towards the outside. Once you're happy, return the cake to the fridge to set.

18 Once set, take it out and enjoy with your family and friends. You can store this cake up to 2–3 days in the fridge. If you have cut the cake already, cover the cut side with cling film to stop it from drying out.

Chocolate piñata cake

WITH BISCUIT BUTTERCREAM AND RAINBOW BUTTERCREAM DECORATIONS

Piñata cake or, as I call it, a surprise cake, is perfect for a proper celebration. It adds an extra element of excitement along with the love and joy of cutting a cake. The first time I made a piñata cake was for one of my colleagues, Julia – I used to borrow piping nozzles from her in pre-*Bake Off* days). It was the cake I made before she went on maternity leave. You might be wondering, why piñata cake? It is because she didn't want to know whether she was expecting a baby boy or a girl. It was a nice surprise for her – both the cake and the baby!

Serves ✿ 8–10

Bake 🖐 45–60 minutes

Ingredients

For the chocolate and cookie cake

85g (3oz) cocoa powder
120ml (4fl oz) warm whole (full-fat) milk
500g (1lb 2 oz) dark brown sugar
170g (6oz) unsalted butter
5 medium free-range eggs
270g (9½oz) self-raising (self-rising) flour
½ teaspoon baking powder
50g (1¾oz) gingernut biscuits, coarsely crushed
80g (2¾ oz) chocolate sandwich biscuits, coarsely crushed

For the biscuit buttercream

1½ batches Swiss Meringue Buttercream (page 34)
100g (3½oz) chocolate sandwich biscuits, finely crushed
50g (1¾oz) gingernut biscuits, finely crushed

For the rainbow buttercream

½ batch Swiss Meringue Buttercream (page 34)
red, orange, yellow, green, blue and purple food colouring gel

For the filling

200g (7oz) Smarties (or other sweets/candies)

RECIPE CONTINUES NEXT PAGE ➡➡

Method

To make the chocolate and cookie cake

1. Preheat the oven to 180°C/160°C fan/350°F/gas mark 4. Grease three 15cm cake tins with butter and line with baking paper.

2. In a mixing bowl, whisk together the cocoa and warm milk using an electric whisk until you have a thick paste.

3. Add the remaining cake ingredients in the order listed and whisk for 1 minute until thoroughly combined.

4. Divide the mixture evenly between the prepared tins and bake for 40–45 minutes, or until a skewer inserted into the middle comes out clean.

5. Remove from the oven and let the cakes cool in their tins for 5–10 minutes, then transfer to a wire rack to cool completely.

To make the biscuit buttercream

6. Add the crushed biscuits to the buttercream and whisk to combine. Set aside.

To make the rainbow buttercream

7. Divide the buttercream equally between six bowls. Add a different food colouring to each bowl.

8. Place a large piping bag fitted with a star nozzle inside a large glass. Fold the ends of the piping bag over the glass to hold it open.

9. Spoon in the different colours of buttercream along the sides of the piping bag in the following order: red, orange, yellow, green, blue, purple. Set aside.

To assemble and decorate

10. When the sponges are cooled, take a 5cm (2in) cookie cutter and use it to cut out the middle of two of the sponges. Set aside the cut-out middles.

11 Use a little of the cookies and cream buttercream to secure one of the sponges with a hole in on a 20cm (8in) cake board or cake stand and place on a cake turntable. Spread a layer of cookies and cream buttercream over the top of the sponge, then place the second sponge with a hole on top.

12 Pour the smarties into the hole, then spread another layer of cookies and cream buttercream over the top of the second sponge and place the third sponge on top, covering the hole.

13 Spread a crumb coat of the cookies and cream buttercream all over the top and sides of the cake and place it in the fridge to chill for at least an hour.

14 Remove the cake from the fridge and ice with the remaining cookies and cream buttercream, spreading it over the top and sides of the cake with a palette knife. Place in the fridge for 30–45 minutes to set.

15 Once set, decorate the top and bottom edge of the cake by piping rainbow buttercream kisses. Return it in the fridge to chill and set the buttercream decorations.

16 This can be kept in the fridge for a couple of days. Remember to take the cake out of the fridge a couple of hours before serving.

Triple chocolate collarcake

WITH CHOCOLATE SCULPTURE DECORATIONS

Serves ✿ 16–18

Bake ✋ 1 hour–1 hour 15 minutes

Ingredients

For the chocolate cake

400g (14oz) salted butter, plus extra
   for greasing
350g (12oz) dark muscovado sugar
8 medium free-range eggs
zest of 4 large oranges
400g (14oz) self-raising (self-rising)
   flour
80g (2¾ oz) cocoa powder
100g (3½oz) Greek yogurt
1 teaspoon baking powder
200g (7oz) milk chocolate, melted

**For the white chocolate and
cardamom ganache**

900g (2lb) white chocolate, chopped
300ml (10½fl oz) double (heavy)
   cream
2 tablespoons ground cardamom

For the chocolate collar

250g (9oz) dark chocolate, chopped

For the chocolate sculpture

500g (1lb 2 oz) dark chocolate,
   chopped
edible gold lustre spray

Method

To make the chocolate cake

1   Preheat the oven to 180°C/160°C fan/350°F/gas mark 4.
    Grease four deep 15cm (6in) cake tins with butter and line
    with baking paper.

2   In a large mixing bowl, whisk together all the cake ingredients
    (apart from the melted chocolate) with an electric whisk
    for about 2 minutes until light and fluffy. Scrape down the
    sides of the bowl and add the melted chocolate. Whisk
    for a further minute.

3   Divide the batter equally between the prepared tins and bake
    for 40–45 minutes until a skewer inserted into the middle
    comes out clean.

4   Remove from the oven and let the cakes cool in their tin
    for 5–10 minutes before turning out on to a wire rack
    to cool completely.

To make the white chocolate and cardamom ganache

5   Make the ganache according to the instructions for White
    Chocolate Ganache for Filling and Coating a Cake (page 55),
    but using the quantities here.

6   Once cool and almost firm but still squidgy to the touch,
    take the ganache out of the fridge and whisk with an electric
    whisk until paler, fluffier and more spreadable.

To assemble the cake

7   Use a little whipped ganache to secure one of the cakes
    on a 20cm (8in) cake board or cake stand and place on
    a cake turntable.

8   Spoon 2 tablespoons of ganache on top of the cake and smooth
    it out using a palette knife. Top with the next cake and repeat
    until all the cakes are sandwiched and stacked.

9   Coat the sides and top of the cake with a crumb coating
    of ganache, then place in the fridge for about 40 minutes
    or in the freezer for about 20 minutes to set.

10 Once set, remove the cake from the fridge or freezer and use
    the remaining ganache to coat the sides and top of the cake,
    smoothing it out with a cake scraper. Return to the fridge for
    40–50 minutes to set completely.

RECIPE CONTINUES NEXT PAGE ➡

To make the chocolate collar

11 Temper the chocolate according to the instructions on page 75. Measure the height and perimeter of the cake, then cut a piece of baking paper measuring the height x perimeter of the cake. Scrunch the baking paper to give it a textured effect, then flatten it back out.

12 Pour the tempered chocolate on top of the baking paper and spread with a pallet knife. Let it cool for few minutes.

13 Take the cake out of the fridge and place on a turn table. Carefully lift the baking paper with chocolate on and, starting from one edge, slowly stick it on the cake, while rotating the turn table slowly.

14 Return the cake to the fridge and let the chocolate set for 15–20 minutes.

15 After that, take the baking paper off to reveal the cake.

To make the chocolate sculpture

16 Line a 15cm (6in) round cake tin with baking paper. Take an 8cm (3¼in) cookie cutter and line the sides and bottom of the cutter with clingfilm.

17 Place the lined cookie cutter in the middle of the lined cake tin. Spoon some of the tempered chocolate into a piping bag, then snip off the end of the bag and pipe the chocolate into the space between the cake tin and the cookie cutter, with a 1cm (½in) thickness. Transfer to the fridge to set for about 30 minutes.

18 Once set, remove it from the fridge. Lift the set chocolate out of the baking tin and carefully remove the lined cookie cutter from the middle. This will give you a chocolate circle.

19 Repeat this process 2–3 times to make a few more chocolate circles of different sizes using different combinations of cookie cutters. Join the circles together with more tempered chocolate to create a decoration, then place in the fridge to set.

20 Once all the chocolate circles are set, Take them out of the fridge to create the sculpture. First place one of medium sized circle on a baking paper. Place the biggest circle vertically on top. Pipe some melted chocolate at the junction and let it set. If you have freezer spray that will be very handy now.

21 Once the big circle is set, pipe a bit of tempered chocolate on top of the big circle at an angle and place the smaller circle there. Spray the freezer spray to set.

22 Once set, carefully lift the chocolate sculpture and place on the top of the collared cake. Spray parts of the sculpture with gold spray and decorate with chocolate butterflies.

23 This can be stored in the fridge easily for couple of days. Space might be an issue with this type of tall cakes. so you can always take the sculpture off from the main cake and store them separately.

Passion fruit cake

WITH CHOCOLATE MIRROR GLAZE AND A CHOCOLATE COLLAR

I love the combination of passion fruit and chocolate. In this cake the passion fruit sponges are sandwiched with passion fruit curd and dark chocolate ganache. Try to coat the cake with the ganache as smoothly as possible and then freeze the cake for at least a couple of hours. In this way you will get an absolutely straight and shiny edge as you pour the mirror glaze on. Finally decorate it with the chocolate flower and lace collar.

Serves ✿ 8–10

Bake 🍷 1 hour–1 hour 15 minutes

Ingredients

For the passion fruit cake

300g (10½oz) unsalted butter, at room temperature, plus extra for greasing
300g (10½oz) caster (superfine) sugar
1½ teaspoons vanilla bean paste
6 medium free-range eggs
100g (3½oz) passion fruit purée
300g (10½oz) self-raising (self-rising) flour
¾ teaspoon baking powder

For the passion fruit syrup

120ml (4fl oz) passion fruit juice
50ml (2fl oz) water
50g (1¾oz) caster sugar

For assembly and decoration

1 batch Passion Fruit Curd (variation, page 62)
1 batch Chocolate Ganache for Coating (page 49)
1 batch Chocolate Mirror Glaze (page 96)
200g (7oz) dark chocolate
1 Chocolate Flower (page 82)

RECIPE CONTINUES NEXT PAGE ➡➡

Method

To make the passion fruit cake

1 Preheat the oven to 180°C/160°C fan/350°F/gas mark 4. Grease three 20cm (8in) cake tins with butter and line with baking paper.

2 In a large mixing bowl, whisk the butter and sugar using an electric whisk for 5–7 minutes until light and fluffy. Scrape down the sides of the bowl and whisk for another couple of minutes.

3 Add the vanilla bean paste and two of the eggs and whisk for 1 minute. Scrape down the sides of the bowl and add the next two eggs before whisking for another minute. Add the final two eggs and whisk once more until you have a silky-smooth mixture.

4 Add the passion fruit purée and whisk well to combine.

5 Sift in half the flour and fold in with a spoon, then add the remaining flour, along with the baking powder, and mix carefully, trying not to knock too much air out of the batter.

6 Divide the batter equally between the prepared tins and bake for 25–27 minutes, or until a skewer inserted into the middle comes out clean.

7 Remove from the oven and let the cakes cool in their tins for 5–10 minutes before turning out on to a wire rack to cool completely.

8 Combine all the syrup ingredients in a saucepan and place over a medium heat. Bring to the boil for a few minutes, then take it off the heat and leave to cool to room temperature.

To make the chocolate ganache

9 Prepare the ganache according to the instructions on page 49. Once it is almost set, take it out of the fridge and whisk with an electric whisk until spreadable.

10 Put half the ganache in a piping bag and leave the rest in the bowl.

To assemble and decorate

11 Use a little of the ganache to secure one of the sponges on a 20–22cm (8–9in) cake board or cake stand and place on a cake turntable. Drizzle a third of the syrup over the sponge.

12 Cut a 1cm (½in) opening in the end of the piping bag and pipe a circular border of ganache around the top of the sponge, slowly rotating the turntable to help you. Fill the middle with half the passion fruit curd.

13 Place the second cake on top, brush with syrup and repeat the step above. Place the third sponge on top and drizzle with the remaining syrup.

14 Coat the top and sides of the cake with a crumb coating of the ganache from the bowl, spreading it out with a palette knife. Place in the freezer to set for at least 30 minutes.

15 Remove the cake from the freezer and coat with a generous layer of ganache. Use a cake scraper to smooth the sides as well the top of the cake. Return it to freezer for a further couple of hours to freeze before glazing.

16 Once the ganache layer is frozen, place the cake on a chef's ring or a wire rack sitting over a large baking tray. Carefully pour the chocolate mirror glaze over the top. Let the glaze set for 10–15 minutes, then carefully lift the cake, with the help of two palette knives, and place on a serving plate or cake stand.

To make the chocolate collar and decorate

17 Cut a long acetate strip measuring 6 × 65cm (2½ x 25½in) and lay it out on the work surface.

18 Temper the chocolate according to the instructions on page 75 and spoon it into a piping bag. Cut a small opening in the end of the bag and pipe any type of decoration you want on to the acetate. You can go freestyle and just do some swirls, or you can be precise and draw some neat lines and shapes. Once the strip of acetate is decorated, wait for a few minutes until the chocolate just starts to set.

19 Now, working quickly but gently, lift the acetate strip and wrap it around a 22–25cm cake tin. Place the cake tin on a baking tray and transfer to the fridge and let it set.

20 Once set remove the cake tin and gently remove the acetate. Carefully lift the collar and place around bottom of the mirror glazed cake. Decorate the top of the cake with the chocolate flower just before serving.

21 It can be kept in the fridge for a couple of days, but the mirror glaze will lose its shine by then.

Cardamom and kirsch Black Forest gateau

Serves ✿ 10–12

Prep ⊙ 30–40 minutes
Bake ♥ 45–50 minutes

Ingredients

For the Black Forest gateau

250g (9oz) frozen pitted cherries, halved

275g (9¾oz) self-raising flour, plus 1 tablespoon for dusting

6 large free-range eggs

230g (8¼oz) dark brown sugar

300g (10½oz) butter, plus extra for greasing

50g (1¾oz) cocoa powder

2½ teaspoons ground cardamom

75g (2¾oz) Greek yogurt

150g (5½oz) dark chocolate, melted and cooled

For the chocolate bark

100g (3½oz) dark chocolate

For the cardamom Swiss meringue buttercream

1½ batches Swiss Meringue Buttercream (page 34)

1½ teaspoons ground cardamom

For the chocolate drip

100g (3½oz) dark chocolate

2 tablespoons vegetable oil

For the kirsch syrup

75g (2¾oz) caster sugar

75g (2¾oz) water

2 tablespoons kirsch

For the cherry filling

100g (3½oz) frozen cherries, defrosted

200g (7oz) Cherry Compote (page 58)

For assembly and decoration

150g (5½oz) fresh cherries with stalk

Method

To make the Black Forest gateau

1   Preheat the oven to 180°C/160°C fan/350°F/gas mark 4. Grease three deep 15cm (6in) cake tins with butter and line with baking paper.

2   In a small mixing bowl toss the frozen cherries in the 1 tablespoon of flour to coat, then set aside.

3   In a large mixing bowl, whisk together the remaining cake ingredients (except the melted chocolate) using an electric whisk for 1–2 minutes until everything is well combined.

4   Scrape down the sides of the bowl, then add the melted chocolate and whisk for another 30 seconds. Finally, add the flour-coated cherries and carefully fold in to the batter.

5   Divide the batter equally between the prepared tins and bake for 40–42 minutes until a skewer inserted into the middle comes out clean.

6   Remove from the oven and let the cakes cool in their tins for 10 minutes before turning out on to a wire rack to cool completely.

To make the chocolate bark

7   Temper the chocolate according to the instructions on page 75.

8   Cut two long strips of baking paper, each measuring about 50 × 10cm (20×4in). Pour the chocolate on to one of the baking paper strips and spread it out evenly using a palette knife.

9   Leave to sit at room temperature for 5 minutes, then carefully position the second baking paper strip on top of the chocolate. Leave for another 5 minutes.

10 Now, carefully roll up the strip, starting from the short side. Once rolled, place it in the fridge for at least 20 minutes to set.

To make the cardamom Swiss meringue buttercream

11 Make the Swiss meringue buttercream according to the instructions on page 34 and flavouring it with cardamom.

12 Spoon about a quarter of the buttercream into a piping bag fitted with a star nozzle. Spoon half of what remains into another piping bag. Leave the rest in the bowl and set aside until needed

RECIPE CONTINUES NEXT PAGE ➡➡

For assembly and decoration

150g (5½oz) fresh cherries with stalks

To make the chocolate drip

13 Place the chocolate in a microwave-safe bowl and microwave on high power in 30-second bursts until melted, then add the vegetable oil and whisk. Pour the mixture into a piping bag and set aside.

To make the kirsch syrup

14 Mix together the sugar and water in a small saucepan. Place over a medium heat and bring to the boil. Allow to boil for a few minutes, then take off the heat and mix in the kirsch.

To make the cherry filling

15 Mix the defrosted cherries with the cherry compote and set aside.

To assemble and decorate

16 Use a little buttercream to secure the first sponge on a 20cm (8in) cake board or cake stand on a cake turntable. Brush about a third of the kirsch syrup on top.

17 Take the buttercream-filled piping bag without the nozzle and cut a 1cm (½in) opening in the end of the bag. Pipe a circular border of buttercream around the top of the sponge, slowly rotating the turntable to help you, then fill the middle with half the cherry filling.

18 Place the second cake on top , brush with syrup and repeat the step above. Place the third sponge on top and brush with the remaining syrup.

19 Coat the top and sides of the cake with a crumb coating of the buttercream from the bowl, spreading it out with a palette knife. Place in the fridge to set for at least 30–40 minutes.

20 Remove the cake from the fridge and apply another layer of buttercream, smoothing it out with a cake scraper until you have a smooth finish. Return to the fridge for an hour to set.

21 Remove the cake from the fridge and pipe the chocolate drip around the edges of the cake, then cover the top of the cake with the chocolate drip too.

22 Now, remove the rolled-up chocolate bark from the fridge. As you unroll it, it will start to break, which is intended. Take the broken pieces of the chocolate bark and position them in a ring around the bottom of the cake.

23 Finally, use the piping bag fitted with the star nozzle to pipe some kisses around the top of the cake. Complete the decoration by placing a fresh cherry on the top of each kiss.

24 This will keep in the fridge for a few days.

5

MERINGUE-BASED AND GLUTEN-FREE CAKES

I am very new to gluten-free baking, but as some of my colleagues are gluten intolerant, it's something I've recently explored. The cakes and cheesecakes in this chapter use little or no flour and wherever they do, it can be replaced with gluten-free flour. The biscuits used for the cheesecake bases can also all be made with gluten-free biscuits.

Chocolate and coffee opera cake

Opera cakes are named after French operas as they have seven distinctive layers, like the seven acts of an opera. It is definitely one of the most elaborate cakes to make, but very rewarding when it is done. It is important to make sure all the layers are almost of equal thickness, that makes it even more special. I will tell you a secret: I took a version of this opera cake to the audition of *Bake Off*, so you probably realise this cake is very special to my heart.

Serves ✿ 10–12

Bake 🧤 45–60 minutes

Ingredients

For the chocolate joconde

5 large free-range eggs plus
    5 large free-range egg whites
75g (2¾oz) caster (superfine) sugar
225g (8oz) ground almonds
1 tablespoon ground cardamom
1 teaspoon almond extract
150g (5½oz) icing (confectioner's)
    sugar
40g (1½oz) unsalted butter,
    melted, plus extra for greasing
30g (1oz) plain (all-purpose) flour or
    plain gluten-free flour, sifted
30g (1oz) cocoa powder, sifted

For the chocolate ganache

½ batch Dark Chocolate Ganache
    for Filling a Cake (page 49)

For the coffee-flavoured French buttercream

1 batch coffee-flavoured
    French Buttercream (page 32)

For the coffee drizzle

1½ tablespoons instant
    espresso powder
5 tablespoons water
75g (2¾oz) caster sugar

For the mirror glaze

1 batch Chocolate Mirror Glaze
    (page 96)

Method

To make the chocolate joconde

1. Preheat the oven to 210°C/190°C fan/410°F/gas mark 6½. Grease four 20cm (8in) cake tins with butter and line with baking paper.

2. In a large bowl, whisk the egg whites using an electric whisk until they form soft peaks. Add the sugar, 1 tablespoon at a time, whisking continuously until all the sugar is incorporated and you have a stiff meringue.

3. In another mixing bowl, whisk together the whole eggs, ground almonds, cardamom, almond extract and icing sugar with an electric whisk for about 5 minutes until well combined.

4. Gently fold the meringue into this batter, trying to keep as much air in the mixture as possible.

5. Remove a large spoonful of this mixture and place it in a separate bowl. Add the melted butter and mix together, then set aside.

6. Divide the remaining batter equally between two bowls.

7. Add the sifted flour to one of these bowls, along with half the butter mixture, and gently fold in.

8. Add the sifted cocoa powder to the other bowl, along with the remaining butter mixture, and again gently fold in.

9. Divide the mixtures between the prepared tins, so you have two filled with the cocoa mixture and two with the other mixture. Spread them out evenly with a palette knife, then bake for 9–11 minutes until springy to touch.

10. Remove from the oven and let the cakes cool in their tins for 5 minutes before turning out on to a wire rack to cool completely.

To make the coffee drizzle

11. Simply combine all the ingredients in a saucepan over a medium heat for 1–2 minutes until you have a syrup. Cool to room temperature.

RECIPE CONTINUES NEXT PAGE ▶▶

For the chocolate decorations

50g (1¾oz) dark chocolate
handful of chocolate curls
edible gold dust

To make the chocolate decorations

12   Melt 2 tablespoons of the tempered chocolate and use it to coat the base of one of the chocolate sponges. Place in the fridge to set. This will be the bottom layer of the cake

13   Take an A4-sized sheet of acetate or baking paper and pour the remaining tempered chocolate over it. Spread out the chocolate evenly using a palette knife. Leave to set for couple of minutes (or in the fridge for 1 minute), then use the blunt side of a knife to score the chocolate.

14   Now, carefully roll up the acetate or baking paper and place it between two chef's rings. Transfer to the fridge to set completely, chocolate-coated side down, for about 30 minutes.

To assemble the cake

15   Place the chocolate-coated base sponge on a 25–30cm (10–12in) cake board or cake stand and place on a cake turntable.

16   Top with a quarter of the buttercream and spread it out evenly. Place a non-chocolate sponge on top and drizzle with coffee syrup. Spread all the chocolate ganache evenly over the top.

17   Top this with another non-chocolate sponge and again drizzle with coffee syrup. Spread another quarter of the buttercream over the top, smoothing it out with a palette knife. Top this with the final chocolate sponge.

18   Coat the top and sides of the cake with a crumb coating of buttercream. Place in the fridge for 15 minutes to set, then coat with the remaining buttercream. Place the cake in the freezer for a couple of hours to set completely.

To decorate the cake

19   Once the cake is completely frozen, remove it from the freezer and place it on top of a chef's ring.

20   Make the chocolate mirror glaze following the instructions on page 96 and carefully pour it over the cake. Let the glaze set for 5–10 minutes.

21   Once set, use two palette knifes to carefully lift the cake and place it on a serving board or cake stand.

22   Decorate the top of the cake with the tempered chocolate curls.

23   Toss some of the coffee beans in gold dust and use them to decorate the base of the cake, along with some more plain coffee beans.

24   Serve and enjoy with your friends and family. If you can't finish this cake in one day, you can keep it covered in the fridge for up to two days. However, remember that the mirror glaze will lose it's shine.

Pistachio, strawberry and chocolate cake

This is one of the most decadent and rich cakes in this book. A slice of this might easily be found displayed in the window of a French patisserie.

Serves ✿ 8–10

Bake ❦ 30–45 minutes

Ingredients

For the pistachio joconde

4 medium free-range eggs, plus
  4 medium free-range egg whites
50g (1¾oz) caster (superfine) sugar
100g (3½oz) ground almonds
60g (2¼oz) ground pistachios
2 tablespoons ground fennel seeds
1 teaspoon pistachio extract (optional)
30g (1oz) pistachio paste
120g (4¼oz) icing (confectioner's)
  sugar
40g (1½oz) unsalted butter,
  melted, plus extra for greasing
30g (1oz) plain (all-purpose) flour or
  gluten-free flour, sifted

For the strawberry mousse

300g (10½oz) strawberries
  (fresh or frozen)
50g (1¾oz) caster sugar
5 platinum-grade gelatine leaves
250ml (9fl oz) whipping cream
50g (1¾oz) fresh strawberries
  (chopped)

For the chocolate mousse

1 batch Chocolate Mousse (page 50)

For the chocolate ganache

150g (5½oz) dark chocolate
150g (5½oz) double (heavy) cream

RECIPE CONTINUES NEXT PAGE ▶▶

Method

To make the pistachio joconde

1   Preheat the oven to 210°C/190°C fan/410°F/gas mark 6½. Grease three 20cm (8in) cake tins with butter and line with baking paper.

2   In a large bowl, whisk the egg whites using an electric whisk until they form soft peaks. Add the caster sugar, 1 tablespoon at a time, whisking continuously until all the sugar is incorporated and you have a stiff meringue.

3   In another mixing bowl, whisk together the whole eggs, ground almonds, ground pistachios, ground fennel, pistachio extract, pistachio paste and icing sugar with an electric whisk for about 5 minutes until well combined.

4   Gently fold the meringue into this batter, trying to keep as much air in the mixture as possible.

5   Remove a large spoonful of this mixture and place it in a separate bowl. Add the melted butter and mix together, then pour the butter mixture back into the main bowl and gently fold it into the batter.

6   Sift the flour on top of the batter and fold in carefully using a metal spoon or silicone spatula, again taking care not to knock out too much air.

7   Divide the batter between the prepared tins, spreading it out evenly with a palette knife. Bake for 9–11 minutes until springy to the touch.

8   Remove from the oven and let the cakes cool in their tins for 5 minutes before turning out on to a wire rack to cool completely.

To make the strawberry mousse

9   Place the strawberries and sugar in a saucepan over a medium heat. Cover and cook for 5–10 minutes, then take off the heat and blend using a stick blender.

10 Pass the mixture through a sieve to remove the strawberry seeds, then return to the pan and gently warm through.

11 Soak the gelatine leaves in cold water for 5 minutes, then squeeze out the excess water out and add the gelatine leaves to the strawberry purée, mixing well to combine. Leave to cool

12 to room temperature.

For the red mirror glaze

1 batch Coloured Mirror Glaze
(page 96), coloured with red food
colouring gel and flavoured with
2 teaspoons strawberry flavouring

For decorating

1 batch tempered Chocolate Curls
(page 77)
100g (3½oz) fresh strawberries, diced
50g (1¾oz) shelled
pistachios, chopped
edible gold leaf (optional)

13 In a large, clean bowl, whip the cream with an electric whisk until it forms soft peaks. Fold the cooled strawberry mixture into the whipped cream and set aside at room temperature.

To make the chocolate ganache

14 Place the chocolate in a heatproof bowl.

15 Warm the cream in a saucepan over a medium–high heat until it is just about to boil. Pour the warm cream over the chocolate and set aside for 5 minutes.

16 Now mix together thoroughly until combined, then cover with clingfilm, making sure the clingfilm is touching the surface of the ganache. Place in the fridge until cooled completely, but not set.

To assemble the cake

17 Line the sides of a deep 20cm (8in) cake tin with acetate.

18 Place one of the joconde sponges at the bottom, then pour the strawberry mousse over the top. Level it out using an offset spatula.

19 Top the strawberry mousse with the second sponge, then spoon the chocolate mousse over the top and level out. Top this with the final sponge.

20 Place the layered cake in the freezer for 2 hours to set completely.

21 Once set, remove from the freezer and carefully lift it out of the tin. Peel off the acetate.

22 Coat the sides and top of the cake with the chocolate ganache, using a palette knife or cake scraper to smooth the sides. Place in the freezer for another 2 hours until completely set.

To glaze and decorate

23 Prepare the mirror glaze following the instructions on page 96 and let it cool to about 33°C (86°F). Remove the cake from the freezer and place on a wire rack set over a baking tray. Pour the glaze over the top, allowing it to pour down the sides as well. Leave to set for 5–10 minutes, then use two palette knifes to carefully lift the cake from the wire rack and place it on a cake stand.

24 Decorate around the base of the cake with the chopped strawberries and pistachios. If you want to be extra fancy, use some edible gold leaf on the chopped strawberries for some added bling!

25 This can be kept in the fridge for a couple of days. The glaze will lose its shine after a day in the fridge, but the taste and textures will be fine.

Meringue and gluten-free cakes - joconde

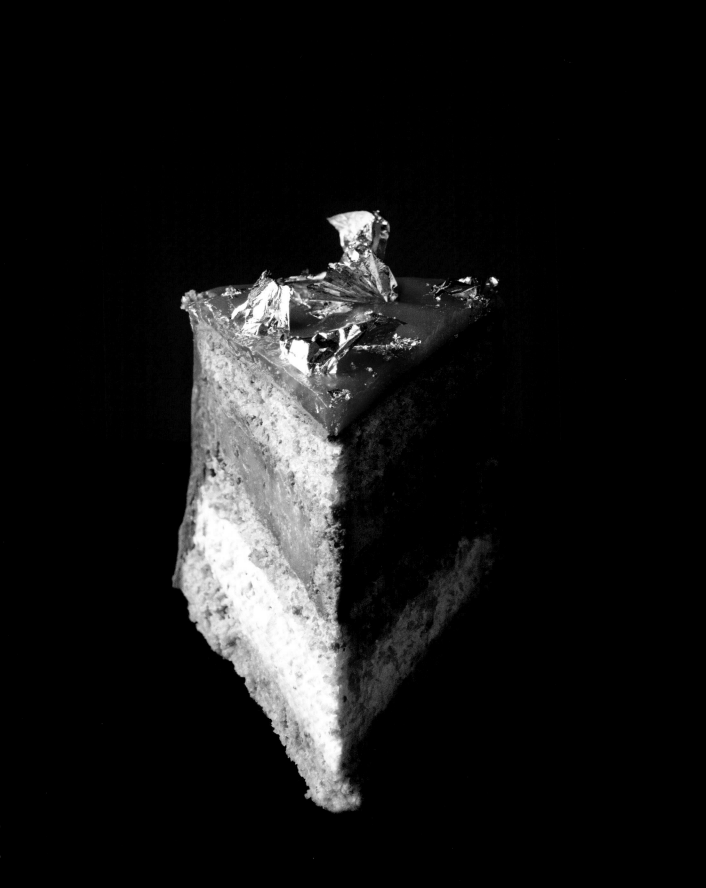

Strawberry and elderflower cream meringue cake

Meringue is my favourite, not only because it is like eating sweet clouds, but also because I often think I am a bit like meringue emotionally: I don't like drastic changes in temperature, temperament or conditions, and I'm sensitive to rude and hateful behaviours, which can result in cracks in my emotional state. Also, if I'm hurt, like meringue, I may end up silently weeping!

This delightful meringue cake is the perfect marriage between the lightness of the meringue and the freshness of the fruits, Let it preach the sermon of summer, sing the song of bright, colourful days and infect you with joy, love and happiness that you can spread to your friends, family and neighbours.

There are a few tricks to making a good meringue. First, make sure the bowl is clean or, more specifically, free from any grease or fat. Rubbing a slice of lemon or a bit of white wine vinegar inside the bowl normally does the trick. Second, whisk the egg whites to soft peaks before you start adding the sugar. And third, add the sugar slowly, a tablespoon at a time, and make sure it's completely dissolved before you add the next tablespoon. When you're done, you will end up with a shiny, thick, edible cloud peaking in your mixing bowl... and, of course, you'll need to test it by holding the bowl over your head to see if the meringue falls out. That's the best part!

My last bit of advice is this: don't be tempted to take the meringue out of the oven as soon as it is done. Turn off the oven and keep the door open slightly with a wooden spoon, then leave the meringue to cool inside the oven for about 1 hour.

Serves 6–8

Bake 🥄 2½– 3 hours

Ingredients

For the meringue

7 medium free-range egg whites
2 teaspoons lemon juice
350g (12oz) caster (superfine) sugar
2 teaspoons vanilla extract
1 teaspoon cornflour (cornstarch)

Method

To make the meringue

1   Preheat the oven to 120°C/100°C fan/250°F/gas mark ½.

2   Take out three sheets of baking paper and draw a 20cm (8in) circle on each.

3   Place each one on a baking sheet, with the pencil-side down.

4   In a large mixing bowl, whisk the egg whites with 1 teaspoon of the lemon juice using an electric whisk. Keep whisking until the egg whites form soft peaks.

5   With the whisk still running, add the sugar, 1 tablespoon at a time. Whisk for 30 seconds after each addition of sugar so that it dissolves and is thoroughly incorporated.

6   Once all the sugar is incorporated, the mix will be glossy and will keep its shape when the whisk is removed. Scrape down the sides of the bowl and sprinkle in the vanilla, along with the cornflour and the rest of the lemon juice. Mix well.

RECIPE CONTINUES NEXT PAGE ➡➡

For the elderflower cream

250ml (9fl oz) double (heavy) cream
3 teaspoons elderflower cordial

For decorating

400g (14 oz) fresh strawberries,
    hulled and quartered
elderflower sprigs, optional

7   Spoon the meringue into a piping bag fitted with a star nozzle and pipe the meringue into the circles on your prepared baking paper sheets. Next, pipe some decorative patterns around the edge of each circle.

8   Once all three circles are piped, bake for 2–2½ hours until baked through. Open the oven door slightly and allow the meringues to cool in the oven for about 1 hour before taking them out.

To make the elderflower cream

9   In a large mixing bowl, whisk together the cream and cordial with an electric whisk until you have soft peaks.

10   Spoon into a piping bag fitted with a star nozzle.

To decorate

11   Once the meringue discs are completely cool, place one of them on a cake stand or cake board. Pipe a third of the cream over the top and scatter over a handful of the strawberries.

12   Carefully place the second meringue disc on top, then pipe on half of the remaining cream. Scatter with another handful of strawberries.

13   Place the third meringue on top and pipe on the rest of the cream.

14   Now arrange the remaining strawberries in concentric circles, like a flower, and decorate with fresh elderflower sprigs, if available.

15   If you want, you can make the meringue discs the day before and store in an air tight container. Assemble on the day it is needed, as this cake serves so much better when it is eaten on the day it is assembled as the meringue will start to go soft over time. It can be stored in the fridge, but considering the amount of cream used, it is better to have it on the same day.

Hazelnut dacquoise

WITH ORANGE CURD AND CHOCOLATE BAVAROIS

This is a gluten-free version of the chocolate and hazelnut cake (page 115) with a hint of orange and cardamom.

Serves ✿ 8–10

Bake 2 hours–2 hours 45 minutes

Ingredients

For the hazelnut dacquoise

350g (12oz) hazelnuts
30g (1oz) cornflour (cornstarch)
30g (1oz) icing (confectioner's) sugar
6 large free-range egg whites
300g (10½oz) caster (superfine) sugar
1 teaspoon ground cardamom

For the orange curd

1 batch Orange and Cardamom Curd (page 62)

For the chocolate and ginger bavarois

200g (7fl oz) whole (full-fat) milk
2 teaspoons ground ginger
50g (1¾oz) caster (superfine) sugar
4 medium free-range egg yolks
3 platinum-grade gelatine leaves
200g (7oz) dark chocolate, chopped
300g (10½fl oz) whipping cream
3–4 knobs of stem ginger, roughly chopped

For the chocolate ganache

1 batch Chocolate Ganache for Coating a Cake (page 49)

For assembly and decoration

100g (3½oz) hazelnuts, roughly chopped

Method

To make the hazelnut dacquoise

1   Preheat the oven to 170°C/150°C fan/340°F/gas mark 3½.

2   Spread out the hazelnuts on a baking tray and roast for 5–10 minutes until aromatic. Remove from the oven and leave to cool slightly.

3   Weigh out 100g (3½oz) of the roasted hazelnuts and roughly chop, then set aside for decorating later.

4   Pulse the remaining hazelnuts in a food processor with the cornflour and icing sugar until coarsely ground. Make sure not to grind them too finely, or the nuts will release the oil and form a paste.

5   Reduce the oven temperature to 145°C/125°C fan/ 295°F/gas mark 1½ .

6   Take two pieces of baking paper. Draw two 20cm (8in) circles on one of them, and one circle of the same size on the other. Use the marked baking paper to line two baking sheets, placing the baking paper pencil-side down.

7   In a large, clean bowl, whisk the egg whites with an electric whisk until they form soft peaks. Start adding the caster sugar, 1 tablespoon at a time, whisking all the while to ensure the sugar is thoroughly incorporated. You should end up with a nice, thick, glossy meringue.

8   Gently fold in the ground cardamom, followed by the ground nut mixture, taking care not to knock too much air out of the meringue. You may find it easier to add this in two batches.

9   Spoon the meringue into a large piping bag and cut a 1cm (½in) opening in the end of the piping bag. Pipe the meringue onto one of your baking paper circles, starting in the centre and spiralling outwards until you reach the edge of the template. Repeat for the other two circles.

10 Bake the meringues for about 1¼–1½ hours, then turn off the oven and leave the meringues inside the oven to cool for a few hours, with the door ajar.

To make the chocolate and ginger bavarois

11 In a small saucepan, warm the milk and ground ginger over a medium heat until just about to boil. Take off the heat.

RECIPE CONTINUES NEXT PAGE ▶▶

12   In a mixing bowl, whisk together the sugar and egg yolks until pale and thick.

13   Pour the warm milk over the egg mixture and whisk to combine, then pour the mixture back into the saucepan. Stir continuously for 7–10 minutes as it starts to thicken, being very careful not to let it boil.

14   When the mixture is thick enough to coat the back of a spoon, take it off the heat.

15   Meanwhile, soak the gelatine leaves in cold water for 5–10 minutes, then squeeze out the excess water and add the leaves to the custard. Stir well to ensure the gelatine leaves are incorporated.

16   Place the chocolate in a heatproof bowl and strain the custard through a sieve and into the bowl. Leave to sit for 5–10 minutes to let the chocolate melt, then whisk well to make a smooth chocolate custard. Leave it to cool down a bit (preferably to room temperature).

17   Meanwhile, whisk the whipping cream in a large bowl until you have soft peaks.

18   When the chocolate custard is almost at room temperature, start folding in the whipped cream, adding it in two or three stages. Finally, fold in the chopped stem ginger and set aside to cool.

To assemble and decorate

19   Line the sides of a 20cm (8in) cake tin or ring with acetate.

20   Place one of the dacquoise at the bottom of the tin. Spread a couple of tablespoons of the orange and cardamom curd on top, smoothing it out evenly.

21   Spoon over half the bavarois and smooth out using a palette knife, then place the second dacquoise on top. Top with the remaining curd, followed by the rest of the bavarois, then place the last dacquoise on top. Transfer the cake to the freezer to set for a couple of hours.

22   Once set, take it out of the freezer and carefully remove it from the cake tin or ring and peel off the acetate.

23   Coat the sides of the cake using 3–4 tablespoons of the chocolate ganache and smooth using a palette knife or a cake scraper. Place it in the fridge to set for about 10–15 minutes.

24   Whisk half the remaining ganache until it is light brown in colour and spoon in a piping bag fitted with a star nozzle.

25   Once the cake is set, take it out of the freezer and coat the sides with the reserved chopped roasted hazelnuts. You want the sides to be completely covered with hazelnuts. all over the top of the cake. You can alternate between the kisses of non whisked star shaped kisses and whisked ganache plain kisses for a contrast.

26   This can be kept in the fridge for couple of days, but it tastes best when enjoyed within the first few days.

Walnut dacquoise

WITH COFFEE PASTRY CRÈME AND WHIPPED MOCHA GANACHE

If you like coffee and walnut cake, you will like this walnut dacquoise with coffee pastry crème. The sweetness of the meringue-based dacquoise beautifully complements the bitterness of walnut, a beautiful cake perfect for any occasion.

Serves ✿ 8–10

Bake 🧤 2 hours–2 hours 45 minutes

Ingredients

For the walnut dacquoise

225g (8oz) walnuts
30g (1oz) icing (confectioner's) sugar
30g (1oz) cornflour (cornstarch)
3 tablespoons instant
   espresso powder
6 large free-range egg whites
300g (10½oz) caster (superfine)
   sugar

For the coffee pastry crème

300g (10½fl oz) whole (full-fat) milk
2tbsp instant expresso
1tsp ground cinnamon
¼tsp ground nutmeg
4 large free-range egg yolks
30g (1oz) cornflour
50g (1¾oz) caster sugar
90g (1¼oz) cold salted butter, cubed

For the whipped mocha ganache

300g (10½fl oz) double (heavy) cream
5 tablespoons instant
   espresso powder
300g (10½oz) dark chocolate,
   chopped

For assembly and decoration

handful of roasted coffee beans
1 batch tempered Chocolate Curls
   (page 77)

RECIPE CONTINUES NEXT PAGE ▶▶

Method

For the walnut dacquoise

1. Preheat the oven to 170°C/150°C fan/340°F/gas mark 3½.

2. Spread out the walnuts on a baking tray and roast for 5–10 minutes until aromatic. Remove from the oven and leave to cool slightly.

3. Pulse the walnuts in a food processor with the icing sugar and cornflour until coarsely ground. Be sure not to grind too finely, or the nuts will release oil and form a paste.

4. Reduce the oven temperature to 145°C/125°C fan/295°F/gas mark 1½ .

5. Take two pieces of baking paper. Draw two 20cm (8in) circles on one of them, and one circle of the same size on the other. Use the marked baking paper to line two baking sheets, placing the baking paper pencil-side down.

6. In a large, clean bowl, whisk the egg whites with an electric whisk until they form soft peaks. Start adding the caster sugar, 1 tablespoon at a time, whisking all the while to ensure the sugar is thoroughly incorporated. You should end up with a nice, thick, glossy meringue.

7. Gently fold in the ground nut mixture, taking care not to knock too much air out of the meringue. You may find it easier to add this in two batches.

8. Spoon the meringue into a large piping bag and cut a 1cm (½in) opening in the end of the piping bag. Pipe the meringue onto one of your baking paper circles, starting in the centre and spiralling outwards until you reach the edge of the template. Repeat for the other two circles.

9. Bake the meringues for about 1¼–1½ hours, then turn off the oven and leave the meringues inside the oven to cool for a few hours, with the door ajar.

To make the coffee pastry crème

10. In a small mug or bowl, mix 100ml (3½fl oz) of the milk with the instant espresso powder. Pour the remaining milk into a saucepan and place over a medium heat. Add the cinnamon and nutmeg, along with the espresso-and-milk mixture, and bring almost to the boil, taking it off the heat just before it boils.

11 In a mixing bowl, whisk together the egg yolks, sugar and cornflour with an electric whisk until pale and fluffy

12 Slowly pour the milk into the mixing bowl, whisking all the while, then transfer the mixture back into the saucepan and place over a medium heat, stirring continuously. After about 7–10 minutes, the mixture will start to thicken. At this point, whisk vigorously using a balloon whisk to achieve a smooth, silky consistency. Remove from the heat.

13 Now, add the coffee extract, then slowly whisk in the cubed butter until combined.

14 Pour the coffee pastry crème into a heatproof bowl and cover with clingfilm, making sure the clingfilm is touching the surface of the cream. Transfer to the fridge to cool completely.

To make the whipped mocha ganache

15 Warm the cream and coffee in a saucepan over a medium heat until just about to boil, then take off the heat.

16 Place the chocolate in a heatproof bowl and pour the warm cream mixture over the top. Leave to stand for 5 minutes, then whisk to create a smooth ganache. Cover with clingfilm, making sure the clingfilm is touching the surface of the ganache, and place in the fridge to cool completely.

17 Once cooled, remove from the fridge and whisk using an electric whisk until lighter in colour and more spreadable. Spoon a third of the ganache into a piping bag and set aside to be used later.

To assemble and decorate

18 Remove the coffee pastry crème from the fridge and whisk until soft and spreadable. Transfer it into a piping bag.

19 Use ganache to secure one of the dacquoise on a 25–30cm (10–12in) cake board or cake stand and place on a cake turntable. Spoon 1 tablespoon of the ganache on top and spread it out. Pipe a ring of ganache around the edge of the dacquoise and fill the inside of the ring with coffee pastry creme. Place the second dacquoise on top.

20 Repeat the process above for the next layer, then top with the third dacquoise.

21 Coat the cake with a couple of tablespoons of the remaining ganache, smoothing the sides with a palette knife or cake scraper. Place in the fridge for 30–60 minutes for the ganache to set.

22 Once set, take the cake out of the fridge. Fill a piping bag fitted with petal nozzle with the remaining ganache. Pipe lines of ganache by touching the wider side of the piping nozzle to the base of the cake. Cover the top of the cake with piped three-dimensional lines of ganache.

23 Keep chilled; remove from the fridge a few hours before serving.

Mixed summer berry and lime cheesecake

Much as I love the flavours of autumn, you can't beat the freshness and abundance of summer. This zesty cheesecake captures just that, filled with the memories of the bright, warm and cheerful days of glorious sunshine! The main purpose of using two types of biscuit for the crust is to add extra flavour rather than just using the traditional digestives. In this recipe, I complement the fruity and floral flavours with the subtle, nutty taste of oat biscuits. However, if you like a bit of warmth, you can always replace them with the same quantity of gingernuts. The cheese filling for this cake is very simple: cream and mascarpone are whisked together, creating a smooth, velvety base – perfect for adding flavours to. The one thing to remember is to be gentle as you stir in the fruit purée to ensure you keep the volume and lightness intact.

Serves ✿ 6–8

Ingredients

For the biscuit base

70g (2½ oz) oat biscuits (you can use a gluten-free alternative)

70g (2½ oz) digestive biscuits (you can use a gluten-free alternative)

50g (1¾oz) salted butter, melted, plus extra for greasing

For the lime cheesecake layer

150g (5½oz) mascarpone, room temperature

100ml (3½fl oz) double (double) cream, room temperature

zest of 2 limes and juice of 1

For the summer berry cheesecake layer

250g (9oz) mixed summer berries, such as strawberries, blueberries and blackberries, plus extra to decorate

25g (1oz) caster sugar

3 platinum-grade gelatine leaves

100g (3½oz) mascarpone

70ml (2½fl oz) double cream

Method

To make the base

1   Line a deep 15cm (6in) cake tin with butter. Place a 15cm (6in) baking paper disc at the bottom and line the sides of the baking tin with acetate.

2   Put both types of biscuit in a food processor and whizz to a coarse crumb. Alternatively, put the biscuits in a freezer bag, making sure you squeeze out all the air, then crush them using a rolling pin.

3   Transfer the crushed biscuits to a mixing bowl and stir in the melted butter.

4   Press the mixture into the base of the prepared tin, levelling it out with the back of a spoon.

5   Chill in the fridge for 30 minutes to set.

To make the lime cheesecake layer

6   In a mixing bowl, whisk together the mascarpone and cream using an electric whisk until stiff peaks form. Whisk in the lime zest and juice. Spoon the mixture on top of the biscuit base and level carefully using an offset spatula. Return to the fridge to set for at least 30 minutes, ideally 1 hour.

To make the berry chocolate cheesecake layer

7   Place the berries in a bowl and use a stick blender to blend them to a purée. Transfer to a saucepan over a medium heat. Add the sugar and bring to the boil, gently stirring to dissolve the sugar. Boil for 2–3 minutes, then remove from the heat and set aside.

RECIPE CONTINUES NEXT PAGE ▶▶

For the mixed berry jelly layer

3 platinum-grade gelatine leaves
250ml (9fl oz) cranberry and
  raspberry juice
100g (3½oz) strawberry jam

Variation

White chocolate pairs exceptionally
well with summer berries, but if you
are feeling experimental, you can
travel to the tropics by incorporating
mango and passion fruit.

8   Soak the gelatine leaves in a bowl of cold water for 5 minutes,
    then remove them from the water, squeezing to remove any
    excess liquid. Add them to the berry mixture, stirring well
    to dissolve. Set aside and leave to cool to room temperature.

9   In a mixing bowl, whisk together the mascarpone and cream
    using an electric whisk until stiff peaks form. When the berry
    mixture has reached room temperature, slowly fold half of it into
    the mascarpone and cream mixture. Once combined, carefully
    fold in the remaining berry mixture. Pour this over the now-set
    white chocolate layer and smooth the top. Return to the fridge
    for at least another hour to set.

To make the mixed berry jelly layer

10 Soak the gelatine leaves in cold water for 5–10 minutes.

11 Meanwhile, combine the juice and jam in a small saucepan
    over a medium heat, mixing well. When the mixture comes
    to the boil, remove from the heat.

12 Lift the gelatine leaves out of the water and squeeze to remove
    any excess liquid. Add them to the juice and jam mixture,
    stirring well to dissolve. Set aside until the mixture comes
    to room temperature.

13 Once at room temperature, slowly pour the mixture over
    the berry cheesecake layer using a ladle.

14 Return to the fridge to set for another 4 hours,
    or preferably overnight.

To decorate

15 Just before serving, decorate the cheesecake with fresh berries.

Kiwi fruit, lime and passion fruit cheesecake

This cake has a hidden passion-fruit layer which, along with the kiwi fruit and lime jelly, gives a fruity tang to cut through the richness of the cheesecake filling. A slice of this cake with the yellow and green jelly reminds me of summer; it's beautiful both to look at and to taste.

Serves ✿ 6–8

Ingredients

For the biscuit base

150g (5½oz) digestive biscuits (you can use a gluten-free alternative)
50g (1¾oz) unsalted butter, melted, plus extra for greasing
zest of 1 lime

For the passion fruit and lime gelée

2 platinum-grade gelatine leaves
190g (6¾oz) passion fruit purée
30g (1oz) caster (superfine) sugar
zest and juice of 1 lime

For the cream cheese filling

4 platinum-grade gelatine leaves
200ml (7floz) double (heavy) cream
1 teaspoon vanilla paste
100g (3½oz) caster sugar
350g (12oz) cream cheese
100g (3½oz) mascarpone

For assembling

3 kiwi fruit, peeled and sliced into half-moons

For the kiwi fruit jelly

2 platinum-grade gelatine leaves
200g (7oz) kiwi fruit purée
zest and juice of 2 limes
50g (1¾oz) caster sugar

For decoration

edible flowers
seeds from ½ pomegranate
2–3 kiwi fruit, peeled and sliced

RECIPE CONTINUES NEXT PAGE ➡➡

Method

To make the biscuit base

1. Grease the base of a 15cm (6in) loose-bottom cake tin with butter and line with a circle of baking paper. Line the sides with a long strip of acetate.

2. Blitz the biscuits in a food processor until you have fine crumbs. Add the melted butter and lime zest and pulse until it starts to clump together.

3. Transfer the mixture into the prepared tin and spread it evenly over the base using the back of a spoon.

4. Use the base of a glass to make sure the biscuit layer is level, then place it in the fridge to set for at least 30 minutes while you prepare the fillings.

To make the passion fruit gelée

5. Line a 13cm (5in) cake tin with clingfilm.

6. Soak the gelatine leaves in cold water for 5 minutes.

7. In a saucepan, combine the passion fruit purée, sugar and lime zest and juice and place over a medium heat. Bring to the boil, then take off the heat.

8. Squeeze any excess water out of the gelatine leaves and add them to the passion fruit mixture. Whisk well to dissolve all the gelatine.

9. Pour the mixture into the prepared tin, then place in the freezer to set for about 3–4 hours.

To make the cream cheese filling

10. Once the gelée layer is set, you can start preparing the cream cheese filling.

11. Soak the gelatine leaves in cold water for 5–10 minutes.

12. In a saucepan, combine the double cream, vanilla and sugar. Place over a medium heat and bring to the boil. Once the mixture starts to boil, take the pan off the heat and set aside for 5 minutes. Squeeze any excess water out of the gelatine leaves and add them to the cream. Whisk to dissolve completely, then cover and leave to cool to room temperature.

13   In a mixing bowl, whisk together the cream cheese and mascarpone using an electric whisk until smooth. Once the cream has cooled, pour it into the cheese mixture and whisk to combine.

To assemble

14   Remove the tin containing the biscuit base from the fridge. Arrange half the kiwi fruit slices in a ring around the edge, against the acetate, with their straight edges touching the biscuit base.

15   Now add the remaining kiwi fruit slices above these, this time the other way up, with their straight edges pointing upwards.

16   Spoon half the cream cheese mixture into the tin, then take the passion fruit gelée out of the freezer. Carefully remove it from its tin and place it on top of the cream cheese layer. Cover the gelée with the rest of the cream cheese filling.

17   Place in the fridge for 2–3 hours to set.

To make the kiwi fruit jelly

18   Soak the gelatine leaves in a bowl of cold water for 5–10 minutes.

19   Combine the remaining jelly ingredients in a saucepan over a medium heat and bring to the boil. Take the pan off the heat. Squeeze the excess water out of the gelatine leaves and whisk them into the kiwi fruit mixture. Cover, then leave to cool to room temperature.

20   Once the cream cheese layer is almost set, very carefully spoon the kiwi fruit jelly mixture on to top, then return the cheesecake to the fridge for 3–4 hours or preferably overnight to set completely.

To decorate

21   Once all the layers have set, take the cheesecake out of the tin and carefully remove the acetate.

22   Decorate the top with kiwi fruit slices.

23   This cheesecake can be left in the fridge for up to a day.

Fraisier cheesecake with spiced jam jelly

This is my interpretation of the famous gateau fraisier in cheesecake form. It has an oat biscuit base with a white chocolate and cream cheese filling with fresh strawberries embedded and topped with spiced strawberry jelly. If you or your friends are gluten intolerant, this will be the perfect treat to enjoy during the summer.

Serves ✿ 8–10

Bake 🍴 10–15 minutes

Ingredients

For the biscuit base

160g (5¾oz) oat biscuits
75g (2¾oz) unsalted butter, melted, plus extra for greasing
zest of 1 lemon

For the cheesecake filling

200g (7oz) white chocolate, chopped
3 platinum-grade gelatine leaves
150ml (5fl oz) double (heavy) cream
1 teaspoon ground cardamom
250g (9oz) cream cheese

For assembly

10–12 medium-sized strawberries, hulled and halved vertically
90g (3¼oz) strawberries, hulled and chopped

For the spiced jam jelly

2 platinum-grade gelatine leaves
150g (5½oz) strawberry jam
150g (5½oz) strawberry purée
¼ teaspoon chilli powder
¼ teaspoon ground cumin
½ teaspoon mustard powder
½ teaspoon ground fennel

For decoration

200g (7oz) strawberries
edible flowers

Method

To make the biscuit base

1   Grease the base of a 15cm (6in) loose-bottomed cake tin with butter and line with a circle of baking paper. Line the sides with a long strip of acetate or foil.

2   Put all the biscuits in a freezer bag, making sure there is no excess air inside the bag. With a rolling pin, smash the biscuits until you get fine crumbs.

3   In a mixing bowl, mix the biscuit crumbs with the melted butter and stir in the lemon zest. Transfer the mixture to the prepared tin and spread it evenly over the base with the back of a spoon, pressing down firmly.

4   Chill in the fridge for 30 minutes.

To make the cheesecake filling

5   Place the chopped white chocolate in a microwave-safe bowl and microwave on high in 30-second bursts until melted. Once melted, cover and set aside to cool completely.

6   Soak the gelatine leaves in cold water for 5–10 minutes.

7   In a saucepan over a medium heat, heat the double cream and ground cardamom until just about to boil. Take the pan off the heat.

8   Squeeze the gelatine leaves to remove any excess water and add them to the cream. Leave to sit for 5 minutes, then whisk well to dissolve the gelatine. Cover and leave to cool to room temperature.

9   In a large bowl, whisk the cream cheese using an electric whisk until it is smooth. Once the cream mixture has reached room temperature, add it to the bowl with the cream cheese, whisking continuously. Finally, add the cooled melted white chocolate and whisk again until well combined.

To assemble

10   Remove the tin containing the biscuit base from the fridge. Arrange the strawberries in a ring around the edge, with their cut sides against the acetate or foil and their pointed ends upwards.

They should be sitting close together, forming the shape of a crown. Carefully spoon some of the cheesecake filling around the edges, into the gaps between the strawberries. Then stir the chopped strawberries into the remaining cheesecake filling and spoon this into the middle, smoothing out to form an even layer.

11   Place in the fridge for at least 3–4 hours to set.

To make the spiced jam jelly

12   Soak the gelatine leaves in cold water for 5–10 minutes.

13   In a saucepan over a medium heat, combine the jam, strawberry purée and all the spices. Whisk to combine, and bring to the boil, taking it off the heat as soon as it boils.

14   Squeeze the excess water out of the gelatine leaves and add them to the strawberry mixture. Whisk well to dissolve the gelatine leaves, then leave to cool to room temperature.

15   Remove the set cheesecake from the fridge and carefully pour the jelly on top, then return to the fridge for another 2 hours to set.

To decorate

16   Carefully take the cheesecake out of the tin and slowly remove the acetate or foil to reveal the strawberry decoration on the sides of the cake.

17   Decorate with more strawberries and edible flowers.

18   Keep for no longer than a day in the fridge.

6

TIERED CAKES

Making a tiered cake can be daunting. I remembered how scared I was before making my first one, which was for a Christmas dinner for homeless people in Rotherham arranged by my colleague Kathryn's church. Once I'd made it, though, it gave me an immense amount of confidence, so what I am trying to say is, it may be daunting but give it a go, it will be rewarding.

You need to ensure that the individual cake boards are the same size as the cakes themselves. Also, if going for a fully frosted look, that the sides are frosted beautifully and look straight. To achieve a stable structure, you'll need to use dowels (either plastic or wood), to take the load of the top tiers and ensure the layers below don't collapse under the weight of the second (or third) cake. And remember, where the tiers join can be covered with piping, flowers or other decorative elements.

Autumn celebration cake

WITH WHITE CHOCOLATE MASCARPONE CREAM, FIGS AND BERRIES

This was the first cake I made after finishing filming for *Bake Off*. It was for one of David's church friends, Gary, who was getting married in a very small ceremony. As he and his wife didn't want a huge celebration, there wasn't a cake for the wedding itself. So David asked if I would like to make one, and I said yes. Hence this cake, simple yet elegant just like Gary himself. It's decorated with figs, blueberries, blackberries and rosemary – all very autumnal. I did get the blueberries from the shops, but David's wife Liz brought some foraged blackberries and rosemary for decoration. I feel all these little elements and memories are attached to any cake, making it special for me and for my friends.

Serves ✿ 20–25

Bake 🍂 1 hour 20–1 hour 40 minutes

Ingredients

For the blueberry and cardamom cake

250g (9oz) frozen blueberries
300g (10½oz) self-raising (self-rising) flour, plus 1 tablespoon for dusting
300g (10½oz) unsalted butter, at room temperature, plus extra for greasing
300g (10½oz) caster (superfine) sugar
6 medium free-range eggs
¾ teaspoon baking powder
zest of 2 lemons
2 teaspoons ground cardamom

For the blackberry and orange cake

100g (3½oz) frozen blackberries
50g (1¾oz) dried figs, chopped
200g (7oz) self-raising flour, plus 1 tablespoon for dusting
200g (7oz) unsalted butter
200g (7oz) caster sugar
4 medium free-range eggs
½ teaspoon baking powder
zest of 1 large orange

Method

To make the blueberry and cardamom cake

1   Preheat the oven to 180°C/160°C fan/350°F/gas mark 4. Grease three 20cm (8in) cake tins with butter and line with baking paper.

2   In a bowl, sprinkle the frozen blueberries with the 1 tablespoon of flour. Toss to coat, then set aside.

3   In a large mixing bowl, whisk together the remaining cake ingredients using an electric whisk for 2 minutes, or until light and fluffy. Scrape down the sides of the bowl and whisk for a further minute.

4   Sprinkle the flour-coated blueberries over the batter and fold them in carefully, taking care not to knock too much air out of the batter.

5   Divide the batter between the prepared tins and bake for 30–35 minutes until a skewer inserted into the middle comes out clean.

6   Remove from the oven and let the cakes cool in their tins for 5–10 minutes before turning out on to a wire rack to cool completely.

To make the blackberry and orange cake

7   Grease two deep 15cm (6in) cake tins with butter and line with baking paper.

8   In a bowl, sprinkle the blackberries and figs with the 1 tablespoon of flour. Toss to coat, then set aside.

9   In a large mixing bowl, whisk the remaining cake ingredients using an electric whisk for a few minutes until pale and fluffy. Scrape down the sides of the bowl and whisk for a further minute.

10   Add the flour-coated blackberries and figs and gently fold into the batter, taking care not to knock out too much air.

RECIPE CONTINUES NEXT PAGE ➡➡

For the white chocolate mascarpone cream

100g (3½oz) white chocolate, chopped
250g (9oz) mascarpone
200g (7fl oz) double (double) cream

For assembly and decorating

2–3 batches White Chocolate Ganache for Filling and Coating Cakes (page 55)
1 batch Blueberry and Lemon Compote (page 58)
½ batch Blackberry Compote (page 57)
500g fresh blackberries
250g fresh blueberries
8 fresh figs
bunch of rosemary sprigs

11 Divide the batter between the prepared tins and bake for 45–50 minutes until a skewer inserted into the middle comes out clean.

12 Remove from the oven and let the cakes cool in their tins for 5–10 minutes before turning out on to a wire rack to cool completely.

To make the white chocolate mascarpone cream

13 Place the chopped white chocolate in a microwave-safe bowl and microwave on high in 30-second bursts until melted. Once melted, cover and set aside to cool completely.

14 Once cool, add the melted white chocolate to a large bowl with the mascarpone and double cream and whisk using an electric whisk until you have a smooth, spreadable consistency.

15 Spoon the mixture into a piping bag and set aside.

To assemble and decorate

16 Prepare the ganache according to the instructions on page 55. Once it is almost set, remove it from the fridge and whisk using an electric whisk until smooth and spreadable.

17 Use a little whipped ganache to secure one of the blueberry and cardamom sponges on a 25–30cm (10–12in) cake board or cake stand on a cake turntable.

18 Cut a 1cm (½in) opening in the end of the piping bag and pipe a circular border of mascarpone cream around the top of the sponge, slowly rotating the turntable to help you. Fill the inside with half the blueberry and lemon compote. Pipe a thin layer of mascarpone cream on top of the compote and spread it out using a palette knife. Carefully place the second blueberry and cardamom sponge on top.

19 Repeat the step above, piping another mascarpone circle and filling it with the remaining compote, then top with the third blueberry and cardamom sponge.

20 Coat the sides and top of the cake with a crumb coating of the whipped white chocolate ganache, then place the cake in the freezer for 15–20 minutes to set.

21 Remove the cake from the freezer and coat with a generous layer of ganache, smoothing it out with a cake scraper for a smooth finish. Return the cake to the freezer to set completely.

22 Repeat the steps above to fill and stack the blackberry and orange sponges on a 15–16cm (6–6¼in) cake board, this time using the blackberry compote and the remaining mascarpone cream. Then, as before, coat the cake with a crumb coating followed by a final coating of white chocolate ganache, and place in the freezer to set.

23 In order to stack the two cakes on top of each other, you will need to reinforce the larger one with dowels. Remove it from the freezer and insert a dowel into the cake, marking the point where it reaches the top of the cake with an edible marker.

Remove the dowel and cut it to size with a sharp knife or scissors. Use this as a template to cut three more dowels to size.

24   Insert the dowels into the middle of the cake at the corners of an imaginary 10cm (4in) square. Pipe a little bit of ganache on top of the dowels, then take the smaller cake out of the freezer and carefully place it on top of the dowels.

25   Decorate the top of the smaller cake with a few whole and halved figs, along with some fresh blueberries and blackberries, and some rosemary sprigs. If you have any leftover blackberry compote, you can drizzle it over the fruit.

26   Where the large cakes meets the small cake, decorate with quartered figs, and more berries and rosemary.

27   Finally, decorate the base of the cake in a similar way. Keep in a cool room until ready to serve.

Chocolate and orange layer cake

WITH SWISS MERINGUE BUTTERCREAM, CHOCOLATE DRIP AND CHOCOLATE SAIL

This is very similar to the first two-tier cake I ever made. White Swiss meringue buttercream, chocolate drizzle and shards and sails make for dramatic effect.

Serves ✿ 15–18

Bake ✋ 1 hour–1 hour 30 minutes

Ingredients

For the chocolate cake

120g (4¼oz) cocoa powder
180ml (6fl oz) warm whole (full-fat) milk
2 tablespoons instant espresso powder
600g (1lb 5oz) dark muscovado sugar
200g (7oz) unsalted butter, at room temperature, plus extra for greasing
6 medium free-range eggs
350g (12oz) self-raising (self-rising) flour
1 teaspoon baking powder

For the orange cake

4 medium free-range eggs
200g (7oz) caster (superfine) sugar
200g (7oz) unsalted butter
200g (7oz) self-raising flour
zest of 2 oranges
½ teaspoon baking powder

For the chocolate drip

100g (3½oz) dark chocolate
50ml (2fl oz) vegetable oil

For assembling and decorating

2 batches Swiss Meringue Buttercream (page 34)
2–3 Chocolate Sails (page 77)

RECIPE CONTINUES NEXT PAGE ▶▶

Method

To make the chocolate cake

1 Preheat the oven to 180°C/160°C fan/350°F/gas mark 4. Grease two 20cm (8in) cake tins and two 15cm (6in) cake tins with butter and line with baking paper.

2 In a mixing bowl, whisk together the cocoa powder and warm milk with an electric whisk until you have a thick paste.

3 Add the remaining chocolate cake ingredients and beat well until fluffy. Scrape down the sides of the bowl and beat for another minute.

4 Divide the mixture evenly between the prepared tins and bake for 30–35 minutes, or until a skewer inserted into the middle comes out clean. (The smaller cakes might need about 10–12 minutes longer as they are deeper. It's also better to bake the larger cakes on the bottom shelf and the smaller cakes on the top shelf.)

5 Remove from the oven and let the cakes cool in their tins for 5–10 minutes before turning out on to a wire rack to cool completely.

To make the orange cake

6 Grease one 20cm (8in) cake tin and one 15cm (6in) cake tin with butter and line with baking paper.

7 Place all the orange cake ingredients in a mixing bowl and whisk with an electric whisk for about 1 minute until well combined. Scrape down the sides of the bowl and beat for a further minute, but take care not to overmix.

8 Divide the batter between the prepared tins and bake for 22–25 minutes, or until a skewer inserted into the middle comes out clean.

9 Remove from the oven and let the cakes cool in their tins for 5–10 minutes before turning out on to a wire rack to cool completely.

To make the chocolate drip

10 Place the chocolate in a microwave-safe bowl and microwave on high power in 30-second bursts until melted. Leave to cool, then add the vegetable oil and whisk. Pour the mixture into a piping bag and set aside.

To assemble and decorate

11 Use a little of the buttercream to secure one of the 20cm (8in) chocolate sponges to a 25–30cm (10–12in) cake board on a cake turntable.

12 Spread another 2 tablespoons of buttercream over the top of the sponge with a palette knife, then place the 20cm (8in) orange sponge on top. Spread 2 tablespoons of buttercream over the orange sponge, and finally top with the remaining 20cm (8in) chocolate sponge.

13 Coat the sides and top of the cake with a crumb coating of buttercream, then place in the freezer to chill for 15 minutes.

14 Meanwhile, repeat the steps above to sandwich and stack the 15cm (6in) cakes, again with the orange cake in the middle. Crumb-coat this cake too, then place in the freezer to set.

15 Once the crumb coats have set, remove both cakes from the freezer and coat with a final layer of buttercream, using a cake scraper to smooth out the sides. Return the cakes to the freezer for 30–40 minutes to set completely.

16 In order to stack the two cakes on top of each other, you will need to reinforce the larger one with dowels. Once set, remove it from the freezer and insert a dowel into the cake, marking the point where it reaches the top of the cake with an edible marker. Remove the dowel and cut it to size with a sharp knife or scissors. Use this as a template to cut three more dowels to size.

17 Insert the dowels into the middle of the cake at the corners of an imaginary 10cm (4in) square. Use a little buttercream to cover the top of the dowels, then take the smaller cake out of the freezer and very carefully place it on top of the dowels.

18 Cut the very end of the piping bag containing the chocolate drip, and use it to drip the chocolate all across both the cakes.

19 Place the chocolate sail on top of the top cake.

20 This can be stored in the fridge for a couple of days. To store in the fridge, separate the top tier from the bottom tier. If you have cut any of the tiers, make sure to wrap the cut side with cling film to stop it from drying out. This cake can be frozen for up to a month. Let it defrost completely before you have it.

Cranberry, white chocolate and cardamom cake

WITH BUTTERCREAM FLOWERS AND FOLIAGE

This cake has a special place in my heart. I created this design for the christening of Brandon, the son of my friends Ben and Jacque. The first time I met them was during one of the *Bake Off* viewing gatherings in 2018. Sounds a long time ago, but it just seems like yesterday. This is exactly how good memories get preserved in our minds. I was only invited to the christening, but wanted to make that occasion memorable, hence I decided to surprise them with a cake too. I am glad to say, little Brandon was very happy with the cake, and went straight for the buttercream flowers. This is what cake does – it makes every event memorable and celebratory.

Serves ✿ 14–16

Bake 🌢 1 hour–1 hour 30 minutes

Ingredients

For the base-tier cake

100g (3½oz) fresh cranberries, roughly chopped

100g (3½oz) dried cranberries

3–4 knobs of stem ginger in syrup, chopped

300g (10½oz) self-raising (self-rising) flour, plus 1 tablespoon for dusting

6 medium free-range eggs

300g (10½oz) unsalted butter, at room temperature, plus extra for greasing

300g (10½oz) caster (superfine) sugar

zest of 3 oranges

2 teaspoons ground cardamom

1 teaspoon baking powder

Method

To make the base-tier cakes

1   Preheat the oven to 180°C/160°C fan/350°F/gas mark 4. Grease three 20cm (8in) baking tins with butter and line with baking paper.

2   In a small bowl, combine the fresh and dried cranberries with the chopped stem ginger. Dust with the 1 tablespoon flour and toss to combine, then set aside.

3   Place the remaining cake ingredients in a large mixing bowl and whisk using an electric whisk for about 2 minutes until everything is well incorporated. Scrape down the sides of the bowl and whisk for 20–30 seconds, then add the flour-coated cranberries and ginger. Gently fold them into the batter.

4   Divide the batter equally between the prepared tins and bake for 25–30 minutes, or until a skewer inserted into the middle comes out clean.

5   Remove from the oven (but leave the oven on) and let the sponges cool in their tins for 10–15 minutes before turning out on to a wire rack to cool completely.

To make the top-tier cakes

6   Grease two deep 15cm (6in) cake tins with butter and line with baking paper.

7   Prepare the batter as above. Spoon the cake batter into the prepared tins, filling them two-thirds full. Bake for 45–50 minutes, or until a skewer inserted into the middle comes out clean.

8   Remove from the oven and let the sponges cool in their tins for about 10 minutes before turning out on to a wire rack to cool completely.

RECIPE CONTINUES NEXT PAGE ▶▶

For the top-tier cakes

50g (2¼oz) fresh cranberries,
   roughly chopped
50g (2¼oz) dried cranberries
2 knobs of stem ginger in syrup,
   chopped
200g (9oz) self-raising flour, plus
   1 tablespoon for dusting
4 medium free-range eggs
200g (9oz) unsalted butter, at room
   temperature, plus extra for greasing
200g (9oz) caster sugar
zest of 2 oranges
1½ teaspoons ground cardamom
½ teaspoon baking powde

For the white chocolate buttercream

750g (1lb 10oz) salted butter,
   at room temperature
750g (1lb 10oz) icing (confectioner's)
   sugar, sifted
750g (1lb 10oz) white chocolate,
   melted and cooled

For the flowers and foliage

1½ batches Swiss Meringue
   Buttercream (page 34)
red, blue, purple, yellow and green
   food colouring gel

For assembly and decoration

300g (10½oz) cranberry sauce

To make the white chocolate buttercream

9   As we're making a lot of buttercream here, you may prefer to do it in three batches, each with 250g (9oz) butter, 250g (9oz) icing sugar and 250g (9oz) melted white chocolate.

10 In a mixing bowl, beat the butter using an electric whisk for 5–7 minutes until light, pale and fluffy. Then add half the sifted icing sugar and whisk well for another 5 minutes. Scrape down the sides of the bowl and add the remaining icing sugar, then whisk.

11 When all the sugar is incorporated, add the cooled melted white chocolate and whisk at high speed for 2–3 minutes. Remember to scrape down the sides of the bowl from time to time.

12 Once you have made all the white chocolate buttercream, separate one-third of the buttercream and colour it blue to frost the bottom tier. Set aside both white and blue buttercream to be used later.

13 Make the Swiss meringue buttercream according to the instructions on page 34. Keep half of it white, and divide the other half between five bowls. Colour four of the bowls with red, , orange, yellow and green food colouring. In the final bowl, combine green and blue food colouring to create a dark green for foliage.

14 Create different flowers with the red, orange and yellow buttercreams (see page 34) and place them in the freezer to harden. If you like, you can fill the piping bag with both white and coloured buttercream to make flowers with two colours.

15 Fit a piping bag with a leaf nozzle and fill it with the green and white buttercream. Fit a second piping bag with a leaf nozzle and fill it with the green buttercream. (If you don't have many leaf nozzles, you can get some piping nozzle couplers. Put them inside a piping bag and then you can use the same piping nozzle for different coloured buttercream.)

To assemble and decorate

16 Use a little of the white chocolate buttercream to secure one of the base-tier sponges on a 25–30cm (10–12in) cake board and place on a cake turntable.

17 Cut a 1cm (½in) opening in the end of the piping bag and pipe a circular border of white chocolate buttercream around the top of the sponge. Fill the buttercream ring with a couple of tablespoons of cranberry sauce. Pipe some more frosting over the top and smooth it out using a palette knife.

18 Place a second sponge on the top and repeat as above, topping with white chocolate buttercream and cranberry sauce before placing the third sponge on top.

19 Use a palette knife to coat the sides and top of the cake with a crumb coating of white chocolate buttercream from either the piping bag or the bowl. Place in the fridge for an hour, or in the freezer for 30 minutes, to set.

RECIPE CONTINUES NEXT PAGE ➡

20   Once set, remove the cake from the fridge or freezer and coat the sides and top of the cake with blue buttercream from the bowl, smoothing using a palette knife or cake scraper. Place the cake in the freezer for another 30 minutes to set completely.

21   Repeat the steps above to sandwich, stack and coat the 15cm (6in) sponges on a 15–16cm (6–6¼in) cake board. This time coat the 15cm cake with white buttercream. After the final coat of buttercream, place in the freezer to set.

22   Next, remove the base-tier cake from the freezer. In order to stack the cakes on top of each other, you will need to reinforce the base-tier cake with dowels. Insert a dowel into the cake, marking the point where it reaches the top of the cake with an edible marker. Remove the dowel and cut it to size with a sharp knife or scissors. Use this as a template to cut three more dowels to size.

23   Take the 15cm (6in) mid-tier cake out of the freezer. Place the base-tier cake on a cake stand and pipe a little white chocolate buttercream on the top of the dowels. Carefully place the 15cm (6in) cake on top.

24   Decorate the sides of both the tiers with buttercream flowers. Fill the gaps between the flowers by piping leaves using the green buttercream. Now use the remaining green buttercream to pipe ivy-like creepers around the sides as well. Use some yellow buttercream to pipe some berries. There is no right or wrong about how to decorate it, so be creative and imaginative.

25   Once you are happy with the design of the flowers and leaves, let the cake set for a few hours in a cool room before serving.

Pistachio, raspberry and yuzu kintsugi cake

This is a Japanese Kintsugi inspired cake. I once told one of my university friends that friendship is like a ceramic vase, once it is broken it is difficult to mend it. And he replied, with honesty, forgiveness, and effort from both sides you can mend it and transfer it to a piece of art. In a way Kintsugi cake reminds me of him, a decoration to see past the flaws and transform the broken pieces to something beautiful!

Serves ✿ 8–10

Bake ♥ 1 hour 15 minutes–
1 hour 30 minutes

Ingredients

For the pistachio sponge

6 large free-range eggs
360g (6½oz) caster (superfine) sugar
360g (6½oz) unsalted butter, at room temperature, plus extra for greasing
250g (3½oz) self-raising (self-rising) flour
200g (5½oz) ground pistachios
2 tablespoons pistachio paste
1½ teaspoons almond extract
½ teaspoon baking powder

For the raspberry sponge

150g (3½oz) frozen raspberries
250g (6½oz) self-raising flour, plus 1 tablespoon for dusting
250g (6½oz) caster (superfine) sugar
250g (6½oz) unsalted butter
4 large free-range eggs
3 tablespoons freeze-dried raspberries, ground to powder
½ teaspoon baking powder

For assembling and decorating

1½ batches White Chocolate Ganache for Filling and Coating Cakes (page 55)
2 batches Raspberry and Yuzu Curd (page 63)
edible gold paint
Wafer Paper Sails (page 93)
Sugar Paste Flowers (page 90)

RECIPE CONTINUES NEXT PAGE ➡

Method

For the pistachio sponge

1 Preheat the oven to 180°C/160°C fan/350°F/gas mark 4. Grease three 20cm (8in) cake tins with butter and line with baking paper.

2 In a large mixing bowl, whisk together all the pistachio sponge ingredients using an electric whisk until pale and fluffy. Scrape down the sides of the bowl and whisk for another minute.

3 Divide the batter equally between the prepared tins and bake for 30–35 minutes, or until a skewer inserted into the middle comes out clean.

4 Remove from the oven (but leave the oven on) and let the cakes cool in their tins for 5–10 minutes before turning out on to a wire rack to cool completely.

For the raspberry sponge

5 Grease and line two deep 15cm (6in) cake tins.

6 In a small bowl, sprinkle the frozen raspberries with the 1 tablespoon of flour. Toss to coat, then set aside.

7 In a large mixing bowl, whisk together the remaining cake ingredients using an electric whisk for 30–60 seconds until light and fluffy. Scrape down the sides of the bowl and whisk for a further minute.

8 Sprinkle the flour-coated raspberries into the bowl and fold them in gently, taking care not to knock out too much air.

9 Divide the batter equally between the prepared tins and bake for 45–55 minutes, or until a skewer inserted into the middle comes out clean.

10 Remove from the oven and let the cakes cool in their tins for 5–10 minutes before turning out on to a wire rack to cool completely.

To prepare the whipped white chocolate ganache

11 Prepare the ganache according to the instructions on page 55. Once it is almost set, remove it from the fridge and whisk using an electric whisk until smooth and spreadable. Spoon half the ganache into a large piping bag and leave the rest in the bowl.

To assemble and decorate

12 Use a little of the ganache to secure one of the pistachio sponges on a 25–30cm (10–12in) cake board on a rotating cake turntable.

13 Cut a 1cm (½in) opening in the end of the piping bag and pipe a circular border of white chocolate ganache around the top of the sponge, slowly rotating the turntable to help you. Fill the circle with a third of the raspberry and yuzu curd, then place the second pistachio sponge on top.

14 Repeat the step above, piping a circle of ganache and filling it with another third of the curd, then top with the third pistachio sponge.

15 Coat the sides and top of the cake with a crumb coating of the ganache from the bowl, then place in the freezer for 30 minutes to set.

16 Repeat the steps above to fill and stack the raspberry sponges on a 15–16cm (6–6¼in) cake board, using raspberry and yuzu curd and white chocolate ganache. Then coat the cake with a crumb coating of ganache and place in the freezer to set.

17 Once the crumbcoat has set, remove both of the cakes from the freezer and coat them with a final layer of ganache. Use a cake scraper to smooth the sides of the cake, then return it to the freezer to set for another 30 minutes.

To create the kintsugi design

18 Typical kintsugi designs are formed after broken pieces of chinaware are stuck back together using gold-coloured clay. Use the handle of a small paintbrush to create some grooves in the sides of the cake. Imagine the cake is a ceramic cylinder that has been broken and you have put it back together. Create the grooves in the places where you imagine the cracks and marks might be.

19 Paint the grooves with edible gold paint, then decorate the cake with the Wafer Paper Sail and Sugar Paste Flowers.

Tiered cakes

Light fruit cake

WITH ROYAL ICING PANELLING AND WAFER PAPER DECORATIONS

This cake is my nod to the glorious past of royal icing decoration. It might be a little tricky to do, considering the piping and the time to set it. But it is the cake for making someone's day truly special. You can potentially use it as a wedding cake too.

Serves ✿ 10–12

Bake 🧤 1 hour 20 minutes–
1 hour 40 minutes

Ingredients

For soaking the dried fruit

550g (1lb 4oz) mixed dried fruit
zest of 2 oranges and juice of 4
50ml (2fl oz) brandy

For the base-tier cake

175g (6oz) self-raising(self-rising) flour,
    plus 2 tablespoons for dusting
4 medium free-range eggs
200g (7oz) unsalted butter,
    plus extra for greasing
200g (7oz) dark muscovado sugar
½ teaspoon baking powder
50g (1¾oz) ground almonds
1½ teaspoons ground cinnamon
1½ teaspoons ground ginger
zest of 2 oranges

For the top-tier cake

3 medium free-range eggs
150g (5½oz) unsalted butter
150g (5½oz) dark muscovado sugar
130g (4¾oz) self-raising flour
½ teaspoon baking powder
40g (1½oz) ground almonds
1 teaspoon ground cinnamon
1 teaspoon ground ginger
zest of 1 orange

Method

To make the base-tier cake

1   The day before you make the cake, place the fruit in a mixing bowl with the orange zest and juice and brandy. Stir to combine, cover and leave to soak overnight.

2   Preheat the oven to 180°C/160°C fan/350°F/gas mark 4. Grease two 15cm (6in) square loose-bottomed cake tins with butter and line with baking paper.

3   Add the 2 tablespoons of flour to the bowl of soaked fruit and toss to combine.

4   In a large mixing bowl, whisk together all the remaining cake ingredients using an electric whisk for 1 minute. Scrape down the sides of the bowl and whisk for a further minute.

5   Scatter two-thirds of the flour-coated fruit on top of the batter, then carefully fold in. Set the remaining fruit aside.

6   Divide the batter equally between the prepared tins and bake for 40–50 minutes, or until a skewer inserted into the middle comes out clean.

7   Remove from the oven (but leave the oven on) and let the cakes cool in their tins for 5–10 minutes before turning out on to a wire rack to cool completely.

To make the top-tier cake

8   Grease two deep 10cm (4in) loose-bottomed square cake tins with butter and line with baking paper. Mix the cake batter as described above, using the reserved soaked fruit, then divide between the prepared tins. Bake for 55–60 minutes, or until a skewer inserted into the middle comes out clean.

9   Remove from the oven and let the cakes cool in their tins for 5–10 minutes before turning out on to a wire rack to cool completely.

10 Prepare the ganache according to the instructions on page 55. Once it is almost set, remove it from the fridge and whisk with the almond extract using an electric whisk until smooth and spreadable. If you are whisking the ganache in batches. add the extract accordingly.

RECIPE CONTINUES NEXT PAGE ➡➡

Tiered cakes

For assembling and decorating

2 batches of White Chocolate
    Ganache (page 55)
1 tablespoon almond extract
blue and black gel
    food colouring
2 batches of Royal Icing (page 70)

11 Divide the remaining ganache in half. Leave one half as it is; this will be for filling and crumb-coating the cakes. Add blue and black food colouring to the ganache and whisk to get a dark blue colour to use as the final coat for both the tiers.

To assemble the cakes

12 Use a little of the white ganache to secure one of the base-tier cakes on a 20cm (8in) square cake board on a cake turntable. Spoon 2 tablespoons of white ganache on top and smooth out using a palette knife.

13 Carefully place the second base-tier sponge on top, then coat the top and sides of the cake with a crumb coating of white ganache. Transfer the cake to the freezer for 30 minutes to set completely.

14 Repeat the steps above to sandwich, stack and crumb-coat the top-tier cakes on a 10cm (4in) square cake board. Place in the freezer for 30 minutes to set.

15 Remove the base-tier cake from the freezer and coat generously with the dark blue ganache, smoothing it out using a cake scraper. Return to the freezer for a further 30 minutes.

16 Next, remove the top-tier cake from the freezer and coat with the dark blue ganache, again smoothing it out using a cake scraper. Return to the freezer to set.

To make the royal icing panels

17 Prepare the royal icing according to the instructions on page 70 and transfer to a piping bag with a 2mm (⅛in) nozzle.

18 Measure the sides of each cake and draw rectangles with the same measurements on a sheet of baking paper.

19 Pipe and decorate the panels with any type of decorations you wish. Leave to dry completely for one day.

20 If you like, you can pipe some more royal icing decorations of your choice on to the baking paper, like the butterfly I have done here. Again, leave to dry completely.

To decorate

21 Once the ganache on the cake are set, take them out of the freezer. Carefully place the top tier on top of the base tier (because fruit cakes are quite dense, this cake doesn't need the extra support of dowels).

22 When everything is assembled, pipe some royal icing or ganache along the edges of the cakes and very carefully attach the panels to the sides of the cake. Use something to gently hold the panels in place. Attach any other royal icing decorations using more royal icing, then leave it all to set for a few hours.

23 Keep the cake in a cool room until ready to serve. You can decorate with fresh flowers just before serving.

White chocolate, lemon and raspberry cake

WITH MODELLING CHOCOLATE FLOWERS

This cake is a celebration of all my favourite cake decorating-techniques. It has the sharpness of fault-line decoration in the top tier contrasted with the fluidity of the drips in the bottom tier and is decorated with modelling chocolate flowers. Of course, instead of making your own modelling chocolate, you can buy it, which makes things a little easier.

Serves ✿ 14–16

Bake 🌂 1 hour 30 minutes–
1 hour 45 minutes

Ingredients

For the lemon cake

6 medium free-range eggs
200g (7oz) caster (superfine) sugar
200g (7oz) salted butter,
  plus extra for greasing
zest of 3–4 lemons
200g (7oz) white chocolate, melted
300g (10½oz) self-raising (self-rising)
  flour
1 teaspoon baking powder

For the raspberry cake

100g (3½oz) frozen raspberries
250g (9oz) self-raising flour,
  plus 1 tablespoon for dusting
5 medium free-range eggs
175g (6oz) caster sugar
175g (6oz) salted butter
150g (5½oz) white chocolate, melted
¾ teaspoon baking powder

For assembling and decorating

150g (5½oz) Lemon Curd (page 62)
4–5 tablespoons raspberry jam
2 batches Swiss Meringue
  Buttercream (page 34)
orange gel food colouring
edible gold paint
3 modelling chocolate flowers

Method

To make the lemon cake

1   Preheat the oven to 180°C/160°C fan/350°F/gas mark 4. Grease three 20cm (8in) cake tins with butter and line with baking paper.

2   In a large mixing bowl, whisk together all the white chocolate and lemon cake ingredients using an electric whisk for about 2 minutes. Scrape down the sides of the bowl and whisk for another minute.

3   Divide the batter equally between the prepared tins and bake for 30–35 minutes, or until a skewer inserted into the middle comes out clean.

4   Remove from the oven (but leave the oven on) and let the cakes cool in their tins for 10 minutes before turning out on to a wire rack to cool completely.

To make the raspberry cake

5   Grease three 15cm (6in) cake tins with butter and line with baking paper.

6   In a bowl, sprinkle the frozen raspberries with the 1 tablespoon of flour. Toss to coat, then set aside.

7   In a large mixing bowl, whisk together the rest of the cake ingredients using an electric whisk for 2–3 minutes. Scrape down the sides of the bowl and whisk for a further minute. Finally, sprinkle the flour-coated raspberries into the batter and fold them in very gently.

8   Divide the batter equally between the prepared tins and bake for 40–50 minutes or until a skewer inserted into the middle comes out clean.

9   Remove from the oven and let the cakes cool in their tins for 5–10 minutes, then transfer to a wire rack to cool completely.

RECIPE CONTINUES NEXT PAGE ▶▶

To assemble and frost the cake

10 Take a quarter of the buttercream and mix it in a bowl with some orange food colouring. Set aside.

11 Place a quarter of the remaining buttercream in a piping bag and set aside. Leave the rest of the buttercream in its bowl.

12 Use a little of the buttercream from the bowl to secure one of the 20cm (8in) cakes on a 25cm (10in) cake board or cake stand and place on a cake turntable. Cut a 1cm (½in) opening in the end of the piping bag and pipe a circular border of buttercream around the top edge of the sponge. Fill the inside of the buttercream ring with half of the lemon curd, then place the second 20cm (8in) sponge on top.

13 Repeat the process above, piping another buttercream ring, filling it with the remaining lemon curd, and finally topping it with the third 20cm (8in) sponge.

14 Coat the top and sides of the stacked cake with a crumb coating of buttercream, spreading it out with a palette knife, then chill in the fridge for 45 minutes or in the freezer for at least 20 minutes.

15 Repeat the steps above to sandwich and stack the 15cm (6in) cakes on a 15cm (6in) cake board, this time using the raspberry jam instead of the lemon curd. As before, coat the top and sides with a crumb coating of buttercream and chill in the fridge or freezer to set.

16 Once the first layer of buttercream has set, remove the cakes from the fridge or freezer and coat each one with a generous layer of buttercream. Use a cake scraper to achieve a smooth finish.

17 Return both cakes to the fridge or freezer to set completely for 20–30 minutes.

To decorate the cake

18 Pipe some orange buttercream around the top of the 20cm (8in) cake and smooth using the cake scraper.

19 Do the same with the bottom of the 15cm (6in) cake. It will create a belt of red buttercream around the top of 20cm (8in) cake and bottom of 15cm (6in) cake.

20 In order to place the top tier on the bottom tier you need to strengthen the cake with dowels. Insert one dowel in the 20cm (8in) cake and mark where it touches the top surface of the cake. Cut the dowel with a pair of sharp scissors. Take that height as a template and cut three more dowels. Insert them inside the 20cm (8in) cake in the corners of an imaginary 10cm (4in) square. Place the top tier cake on top of the dowels.

21 Fill a piping bag with the the orange white chocolate drip. Cut a 2–3mm opening and pipe the drip all across the base of the top tier, encouraging it to drip down the sides of the base tier cake.

22 Decorate with the modelling chocolate flowers before serving.

23 This will keep for a couple of days in the fridge.

Tiered cakes

Pumpkin spice and orange Halloween cake

WITH CARAMEL FILLING AND BUTTERCREAM DECORATIONS

This cake is supposed to look like a pumpkin or an Impressionist's view of a pumpkin. Layering the cakes is straightforward. But then you have to carve the ridges of the pumpkin using a sharp knife. Finally coat the whole cake with a mix of orange, red and yellow buttercream. It is the perfect cake for a Halloween or a Thanksgiving celebration.

Serves ✿ 16–20

Bake ✋ 45–60 minutes

Ingredients

For the pumpkin spice and orange cake

600g (1lb 5 oz) unsalted butter, at room temperature, plus extra for greasing
600g (1lb 5 oz) caster (superfine) sugar
9 large free-range eggs
zest of 4 large oranges
550g (1lb 4oz) self-raising (self-rising) flour
1 tablespoon ground cinnamon
1 tablespoon ground ginger
¾ teaspoon ground nutmeg
¾ teaspoon cloves
¾ teaspoon allspice
100g (3½oz) ground almonds
50ml (2fl oz) whole (full-fat) milk

For the caramel Swiss meringue buttercream filling

1–1½ batches Swiss Meringue Buttercream (page 34)
200g (7oz) Salted Caramel Sauce (variation, page 44)

For assembly and decoration

1½–2 batches Swiss Meringue Buttercream (page 34)
orange, red, yellow, blue and green gel food colouring

Method

To make the pumpkin spice and orange cake

1   Preheat the oven to 180°C/160°C fan/350°F/gas mark 4. Grease four 20cm (8in) cake tins with butter and line with baking paper.

2   In a large mixing bowl, whisk together the butter and sugar using an electric whisk for 7–10 minutes, scraping down the sides of the bowl a couple of times as you go.

3   Once the mixture is light and fluffy, start adding the eggs, two at a time, whisking and scraping down the sides of the bowl after each addition.

4   Once all the eggs are incorporated, mix in the orange zest, then sift in half the flour and all the spices on top of the batter. Mix together on a low speed.

5   Sift in the remaining flour, followed by the ground almonds. Finally, add the milk, then gently fold everything together using a spatula or metal spoon.

6   Divide the mixture equally between the prepared tins. Bake for 30–35 minutes, or until a skewer inserted into the middle comes out clean. Remove from the oven and let the cakes cool in their tins for 5–10 minutes before turning out on to a wire rack to cool completely.

To make the caramel Swiss meringue buttercream filling

7   Make a batch of Swiss Meringue Buttercream, then stir in the caramel and whisk well until you have a spreadable consistency.

8   You will need a further 1½ batches of Swiss meringue buttercream for the decoration and frosting. Take half a batch and divide it between three bowls. Colour the buttercream in each bowl with a different food colouring, so you have red, orange and yellow. This will be used to frost the cake after you have carved it.

9   Divide the remaining buttercream into as many bowls as you need to make the different colours for making the flowers and foliage to decorate the cake. As we're making flowers, I usually divide it into 6–7 bowls and have colours like red, orange, blue and purple, and then have a few different shades of green for

creating interesting foliage. To create different shades of green, just add a little blue for a darker green, or some yellow for a lighter one. It's always a good idea to keep one bowl of plain white buttercream, too, so you can create bi-coloured flowers.

10   Create a set of buttercream flowers following the instructions on page 84, then place them in the freezer for 30 minutes to set.

11   For the leaves, spoon all the different shades of green into different piping bags with and set aside. You will use these at the end to pipe the leaves straight on to the cake with a leaf nozzle.

To assemble the cake

12   Use a little of the salted caramel buttercream to secure one of the sponges on a 30cm (12in) cake board on a cake turntable. Spoon a couple of big dollops of salted caramel buttercream on to the cake and smooth out using a palette knife. Place the second sponge on top.

13   Repeat to sandwich and stack all four sponges with buttercream.

14   Place the cake in the freezer for a few hours, to get it semi-frozen: this will make it much easier to carve.

To carve the cake

15   Now it's time for the exciting part: carving the cake into a pumpkin. Use a 15cm (6in) round cake board as a guide and place it on top of the cake in the middle.

16   Use a serrated knife to trim 1.5cm (¾in) off the top edge of the cake all the way around. Place the cake in the freezer for 30-45 minutes for it to set.

17   Remove the cake from the freezer and place a 30cm (12in) cake board on top. Flip the cake upside down and remove the cake board from what is now the top (and was previously the base). Place the 15cm (6in) cake board on what is now the top. Again use this board as a guide to trim off 1.5cm (3/4in). The cake should now be an oblate shape with both the top and bottom edges trimmed and tapered. For the grooves on the side of the pumpkin, use a small serrated knife to mark 6-8 vertical ridges from top down the sides to the base. Make the ridges about 1–1.5cm (½–¾in) deep. Carefully carve vertical grooves around the cake by making the first cut with the knife at a slight downwards angle then make the second cut with the same technique but angle the knife towards the first cut, so that the piece removed is in a triangular shape. Be careful not to remove any large pieces or cut too deep. Slowly work your way around the whole cake.

18   When you are happy with the overall shape, rotate the cake slowly and smooth any rough or angular edges with the serrated knife.

19   Use the remaining caramel buttercream to apply a crumb coat to the carved cake, then return it to the freezer for 1–2 hours.

RECIPE CONTINUES NEXT PAGE ➡

20 Remove the cake from the freezer and coat with a mix of orange and yellow buttercreams, then smooth the sides of the cake with a small palette knife. If you want you can keep the buttercream a little rough like an Impressionist painting.

21 Fill a piping bag with the red buttercream, snip off the end of the bag and pipe the red buttercream along the pumpkin's ridges. Smooth out using a palette knife, then place in the fridge for 30 minutes.

To decorate the cake

22 Once you are happy with the pumpkin, decorate the top with the buttercream flowers and pipe different type of foliage across the top with your green buttercream.

23 Finally, place the cake on a cake stand and decorate the bottom with some more buttercream flowers and foliage.

24 It will keep couple of days in the fridge.

ACKNOWLEDGEMENTS

Firstly, I'd like to thank my parents who've always supported me in everything I do. My taking up baking, and *Bake Off*, was a shock to them. They knew that I loved cooking but never thought I would be either good enough or brave enough to apply for such a show. My mum has always praised all my cooking. My dad, on the other hand, has always been very honest. If he doesn't like something, he won't touch it. I speak with them every day and find it comforting to share what has happened. Even if they don't understand why I am annoyed or upset, it is good to say it out loud. Thanks so much for making me who I am and for listening to me.

Huge thanks, too, to my colleague David and his wife Liz, who with Sue, Graham, Molly, Sean, Harry and Margaret gave me the family I longed for in the UK. Liz's taste buds are amazing, and it's always a great help to know her opinion on any new recipes I develop. I'd also like to thank my colleagues in the Nuclear AMRC for their constant support and encouragement. You gave me a reason to bake surprise birthday cakes – some of which have made it into this book. I may not have brought in any recently because of COVID rules but normal service will resume soon!

Thanks to the amazing cast and crew of The Great British Bake, who've always been super proud of everything I've done. And the bakers – all 132 of them! I wouldn't have found the courage to apply, or to write this book, if bakers such as Edd, John, James, Nadiya, Sophie, Nancy, Stephen and Candice hadn't gone before me. *Bake Off* has also given me 11 amazing friends from 2018 with whom I share a unique bond. But the list doesn't end there. The *Bake Off* family keeps growing and is very welcoming. Hermine and I became best buddies from the moment we met. We chat most days and I have never met anyone so encouraging and selfless. Along with Steph and her mum, Jane, she has been a huge support when I felt I wasn't good enough and questioned my ability. Thanks for sticking by me and inspiring me to be a better baker every day.

Huge thanks, too, to Judith and her team at Kyle Books for believing in me. To photographer Maja for showing me that 'less is more' and sharing some amazing photography tricks. To food stylist Lottie and her team of assistants for making everything happen.

Also, thanks to Anna from Yellow Poppy. I am not the best person to work with, but thanks for making it easy in the difficult times.

Last but not the least I'd like to thank you for buying this book. I hope it helps your baking and, more importantly, inspires you to experiment and create your own style of baking.

INDEX